ENDORSEMENTS

Reading this book is like watching a God-centered surgeon perform his very own ego-bypass surgery. The importance of this little book is that Pastor Ross' procedure—meticulous, brave, alternately probing and humorous, unfailingly human—applies to anyone who seeks God's will and aspires to integrity. The soul-searching begins in a mundane way. A men's ministry has to be installed. Being in a rural area, men wanted to hunt and fish. Pastor Ross was not naturally of their ilk, but tried to be, and along the way, painfully admitted to himself "I didn't have the stuff," and that a colleague might be more qualified, and being a man who cared about "what God wanted," he asked himself: "Do you love God? Let me just say, if your primary reason for wanting to lead a men's ministry isn't to serve and please God, then you are wasting everyone's time." In this incident Pastor Ross finds the world in a grain of sand and then he delivers the goods: "Pastors are men with egos, insecurities, control issues, and a strong sense of responsibility. All of which can be perverted and lead to unrighteousness." Having put his ego aside, facing his insecurities, weaknesses and fears head on, Pastor Ross finds his way by getting out of the way. In stepping aside, he finds his bearings. The lesson for us all is quietly momentous, in clear fluid prose with a fully human heartbeat and laugh-out loud moments.

If I were a young person seeking a pastorate, or one who lost his way, I would embrace this slim book and its hard-won wisdom from a seasoned shepherd who stands between his flock and the wolves, and who is savvy enough to know that there are wolves without and wolves within, and the good shepherd must be ever wary. If I aspired to be that shepherd, I would make this book my vade mecum.

—William Mastrosimone. An American Playwright
Writer of: *The Beast, With Honors, Extremities, Into the West*

As a former Men's Pastor of a large church, I recognize the fact that a Sr. Pastor has so much on his plate that listening to each of these special interest groups about their passion is simply another thing to be place on his Sr. Pastor plate. Pastor Ross Holtz is a Sr. Pastor and is expressing this same position in his book, *"Are you in the Game?"* Pastor Ross has done an excellent job of describing the how these special interest groups and specifically the Men's Pastor can take on responsibility to assist the Pastor with his plate already being too full. This is an excellent read with practical illustrations of this process from a Sr. Pastor in the trenches. This will also teach the men's leader value lessons to gain the trust of the Sr. Pastor in your church.

—Darrel Billups, Th.D.
NCMM, Executive Director
National Coalition of Ministries to Men

ARE YOU

in the

GAME

or in the

WAY?

a question for pastors and men's ministry leaders

ARE YOU
in the
GAME
or in the
WAY?

a question for pastors and men's ministry leaders

Ross Holtz

REDEMPTION
PRESS

ISBN 13: 978-1-68314-243-0 (Print)
978-1-68314-244-7 (ePub)
978-1-68314-245-4 (Mobi)

Library of Congress Catalog Card Number: 2017934264

DEDICATION

For Joshua's Men at The Summit and the men who lead
and led, Jay and Brad.
And for the Clan Holtz, *Infractus Quod Invictus.*

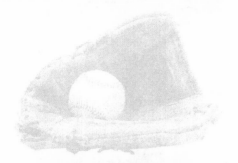

CONTENTS

Part III The Fix

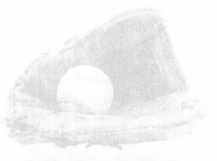

FOREWORD

When I consider a book to read, two primary factors weigh the heaviest for me. The first factor is the subject, and more specifically, the manner in which it is being addressed. The second factor is the author. The primary concern is whether or not the author has the experience to speak with firsthand knowledge. I also consider whether he has earned the right to speak on the subject.

I am very excited about the book, *Are You in the Game or in the Way?* written by Ross Holtz. Pastor Ross is a man who has the experience and has earned the right to speak on the subject of ministering to and through men.

Full disclosure and complete transparency are always good when making a recommendation. For over five years, I have encouraged Pastor Ross to write this book. Few men have the years of experience and the personal engagement in men's ministry with the passion and commitment of this man.

Ministering to and through men is not something Ross does as a ministry task because he has been told it is part of his job description. He has a God-given passion to see men remade in the image of our Father.

Experience matters! Pastor Ross has poured his life into ministry to men; and as a result, he is an avid student of God's Word and how it applies to men to be who God created us to be. He is engaged in ministering to men from the individual man one-on-one, to the church, and to area-wide, regional, national, and international arenas.

Are You in the Game or in the Way? is more than a book to educate us on the mechanics of men's ministry or on how to host a successful men's breakfast. It is one man's journey from being a skeptic to a fully engaged pastor who sees the power of a clear ministry to and through men. Pastor Ross bares his heart and is, at times, brutally honest in a manner with which many pastors and/or men's leaders will resonate. Ross speaks with clarity regarding the relationship between the pastor and men's leader.

For many years, I have had an image in my mind of Ross Holtz. In September 1944, Brigadier General Charles Canham, assistant division commander of the 8th Infantry Division, was sent to accept the surrender of Lieutenant General Ramcke, commander of the elite German 2nd Parachute Division, after the Battle for Brest. When BG Canham arrived, accompanied by several battle-weary soldiers, the German general, upon realizing that the American general was junior to him in rank, asked, "What are your credentials?"

Without hesitating, BG Canham turned, pointing to the battle-tested soldiers with him, and responded, "These are my credentials."

If you need to see the credentials of Pastor Ross Holtz, you need only to look at the battle-tested men he has stood with and who stand with him. Those are his credentials. I know of no man who has better credentials to write this book.

It is also important to know that Pastor Ross Holtz was selected as the "Men's Ministries Pastor of the Year" in 2014 by the National Coalition of Ministries to Men. This award is not given without significant vetting of the man and his impact on men's ministries.

If you have any interest in men's ministry at any level, Ross has given you and me a very special gift. His gift is his own life journey, complete with the joy and the heartbreaks.

In the years to come when pastors and men's ministry leaders list the foundational books in their libraries for men's ministry, *Are You in the Game or in the Way?* will be on their lists.

In conclusion, Ross Holtz is more than my friend—he is my brother-in-arms and one of my trusted battle buddies. His life has impacted and ministered to me since the first day he and I met. I am a better man because of him in my life, and I am convinced this book will help you move closer to being the man you want to be and a better leader of other men.

—Chuck Stecker, president, A Chosen Generation

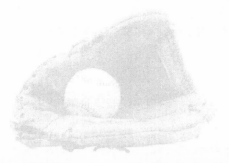

ACKNOWLEDGMENTS

To my publisher, and wife, Athena Dean Holtz, who has lovingly cajoled me into finishing the book. You are helping me write the second chapter of my life. God loves you and so do I.

To my sons, daughter, daughters-in-law, and grandchildren: I am a rich man because of y'all. Through thick and thin we've sloshed on, *Broken, but Not Defeated.* And by God's good grace, we'll stand together through whatever comes.

To my friend, brother, and confidant, Chuck Stecker, who almost every week for several years asked, "How's the book coming?" You are the kind of man every guy needs as a friend, but most never find.

To Brad and Jay, faithful leaders of Joshua's Men. Brad, you pushed me into men's ministry and designed the ministry. Jay, you successfully built on the foundation and have led the men and served the church for more than a decade. You two taught me about ministering to men and have been faithful as warriors for the kingdom. We've stood shoulder to shoulder through some trying times, and you always had my back. I am proud to be your friend and compatriot.

To the people of The Summit in Enumclaw, Washington, especially Joshua's Men, who have walked with me and supported me for thirty years. Such endurance will get you points in heaven.

To Cathy, my late wife, who always said I had a book in me but didn't live to see it published. May you rest in peace in Yeshua's loving arms.

INTRODUCTION

In the last decade or so, we've seen a great increase in ministries to men in the American church. And it is high time. But all is not as it should be. While this is great news, there is a problem that has become evident.

> We've got trouble, right here in River City!
> Trouble with a capital "T" that rhymes with "P"
> And that stands for Pool.[1]

I'll amend that to say, "We've got trouble with a capital "T" that rhymes with "P" . . . and that stands for Pastor!"

---

[1] "Ya Got Trouble," Robert Preston, The Music Man, 1962.

According to Dr. Robert Lewis and many others, the major obstacle in getting ministries to men started is—say it by name—the senior pastor. The problem is simply that the guy who should be at the forefront is often in the way of the program getting off the ground.

Ah, but that isn't the whole story, is it? There is evidence that the problem is often two-sided. There is some room to share blame with the men who would be leaders of ministries to men. So we'll take a look at the problem from both sides.

I have a simple question for both the senior pastor and the men's ministry leader or wannabe:

Are you in the game, or in the way?

Let's talk.

PART I

My History, My Story

1

MEN'S MEN AND ME

If the senior pastor gets behind a men's movement in his church it will happen. Without him, the church will starve for godly men to make a difference.

—Dr. Robert Lewis[2]

I have not always believed that the pastor holds such a crucial role. When I grew up in the church, the formal leadership was always men, but we all knew if anything was to be done, the women, the real power brokers in the church, would have to be behind it.

Men were an add-on in the life of the evangelical church, and they participated at whatever level the women could get them to. It seems counterintuitive, but anyone who worked in

---

[2] Dr. Robert Lewis in a presentation to Reload 14, National Coalition of Ministries to Men.

the church for any time knew it was true. There were exceptions of course, but just enough to prove the rule.

The axiom I grew up with, and experienced in the early days of pastoring, was if it were not for the women, the church would have died sometime after the Civil War. I saw enough proof to believe it wholeheartedly. So not only was I not behind a ministry to men, I wasn't sure we needed one. Hard to believe, but that's how it was. And I can name you many, many pastors who do, or did, believe that same thing.

We tried to draw men in, of course. There were always the construction projects around the church that men would get behind, but on the spiritual plane, it was pretty much the women who made the wheels go round. From time to time we'd try to start men's breakfasts and other kinds of male-oriented events to get them interested, but they were largely short-term ministries that ran for a season and then died an untimely death. As unkind as it sounds, the men who did participate on a more-than-very-casual basis were more likely to enjoy sharing conversation with women than the kind of guys who did more outdoor activities. To continue the stereotype, they were usually more cerebral, bookish, gentle kinds of guys who fit the more sedate life of the church. It seemed to me then, and it still does, that many were men who seemed as if their passion, enthusiasm, and joie de vivre had been surgically removed. Manly was not a term usually attributed to churchmen. That's not a totally fair representation of these "churched" men, but rarely were they the kind of men considered to be a "man's man."

Manly was not a term usually attributed to churchmen.

There were always a few who kept our hopes alive, but then again, they were always slightly suspect. Did they have some kind of secret lives we didn't know about? And, yes, that was sometimes true. They hadn't totally bought in to the passivity the church seems to instill, and sometimes require, in its male participants.

. . . .

In the early eighties, I pastored a church in a small logging town in Washington State. One Sunday on my first fall there, we began our worship service with about fifty women, an old, rather infirm man, and myself in attendance. My question as I went on the platform was, "Did hunting season just start?" The women all nodded in one accord. I quickly learned what was important to the men of the community—and it wasn't the church.

I quickly learned what was important to the men of the community—and it wasn't the church.

> *I wasn't open to becoming one of them. The hard truth was: I didn't have the stuff.*

So I tried having a ministry to hunters. Yeah, well, they weren't the types to sit around, drink coffee, and talk about hunting—they wanted to be out in the woods doing it. My study group of hunters turned out to be a contradiction in terms.

Oh, when we had to roof the church they all showed up with friends and did a great job splitting shakes and carrying them up very tall ladders and nailing them down in grand style. The new roof was a thing of beauty. But the next day they were all too worn out or too disinterested to attend the dedication of the new roof. Once again it was largely the women, a few guys, and me.

I wanted to reach out to them and draw them into the church. They were good men and many were professing believers, but the church life just didn't appeal to them. They were friendly to me and were mostly sympathetic to the church, the only one in town, but evidenced no real attraction to what I was offering.

The problem, it turned out, was not the men of the church and community; it was with me. My passion was the Scriptures and the stuff of books. I was raised in the San Francisco area and had no knowledge of outdoor life. I wanted to recruit them into my life, to the life I saw as the church. I was, inadvertently, attempting to draw them away from their own lifestyles and community to participate in mine. I learned I wasn't open to becoming one of them. The hard truth was: I didn't have the stuff.

2

· ·

THEN CAME BRAD

He said, "Pastor, we don't have a ministry for men here at The Summit. How come?"

I said, "Shut up and go away! We have a ministry that is aimed at men and women, ergo, we have a men's ministry."

It was now a later time and another church. The *he* was Brad Stewart, and my response was only in my head. I'm not dumb enough to be *that* honest to a guy new to our church. But that, as I recall, was pretty much what I was thinking.

I had, over the years, had others suggest the same thing and that was my standard reaction. Who did they think they were anyway? I was the senior pastor and we had a growing congregation. If God wanted a ministry directed specifically to men, He'd give me the instructions and I'd do it. But I was busy and there wasn't time to add something else to an already successful (in my eyes anyway) ministry.

The term *men's ministry* conjured up for me painful experiences of getting up before dawn on a Saturday morning, eating soggy pancakes, and talking about stuff no one cared about. The men were there because their wives thought it would be nice, or out of loyalty to someone. We'd eat our pancakes and make small talk. Then some guy would get up and stumble through a devotional talk, we'd take prayer requests, a couple of guys would mumble through some prayers, then everyone would run for the door to get out of the church and get on with real life.

But Brad was persistent. He wouldn't shut up and I couldn't get him to go away. Oh, man, what was I supposed to do?

• •

I'd met Brad and his wife, Marianne, at another church about six months before. I was there representing the Pacific Northwest District of the Evangelical Free Church of America in a pastor failure issue. During the small talk after the sessions, Brad and I struck up a conversation. I discovered he and Marianne lived considerably closer to the church we'd planted a few years earlier. He was new to that church and admitted, "We don't feel like we're fitting in there."

"You're welcome to come try our church and see if you feel at home," I said. Little did I know the trouble I was getting myself into. Brad and Marianne tried our church, felt at home, and

Chemistry between leaders is essential.

soon afterwards, he started the conversation about our lack of a men's ministry.

Now what was I supposed to do with him? He was a retired senior chief with the U.S. Navy and a graduate of some years of Navigators training. He was a formidable antagonist who didn't take no for an answer.

Well, I didn't outright tell him no, I just put him off indefinitely. That's what most pastors do when we have a person who wants to do something we aren't ready for. We don't say, "No, go away," which is what we're thinking, we just put it off for another day.

I didn't know Brad well and I historically haven't put people into leadership positions before I get to know them well. I believe that chemistry between leaders is essential. So I told him, "Brad, hang around for a while, let's get to know each other, and we'll talk in a few months."

I liked Brad, but the whole men's breakfast thing or running around in the woods beating our chests and shooting things was beyond me.

ARE YOU IN THE GAME OR IN THE WAY?

_____

Fear is a lousy motive for decision making.

In the years following this encounter, I've wondered why I responded that way. *Am I just not a man's man? Am I not spiritual enough or what?*

Then I realized Brad threatened me. He threatened my ministry by pointing out a weakness I didn't want to see.

I wrestled with my reluctance to see a ministry to men get started. *What am I afraid of?*

All pastors experience people coming to them saying, "I'd like to start a ministry to . . ." What they mean is they want the pastor to start such a ministry. As young enthusiastic preachers, most of us fall into that ditch too often. The ministry starts out with a team of excited laymen and soon the poor pastor ends up with another job on his already too-full plate.

But it wasn't only that for me. I'd worked hard cultivating a relationship with the families of our church and I wasn't eager to watch someone else take half of them and "steal" their affections. This has happened too many times in churches not to be considered a real threat.

Fear is a lousy motivation for making any decision concerning the body of Christ. I knew I was going to have to confront my fears. Insecurity is a dreadful thing. Instead of being able to celebrate another man's success, an insecure man becomes jealous and afraid the group is going to see the other guy as better, smarter, more spiritual, and more of a man than he is.

What if the guys like the other leader better?

What happens when a pastor wakes up and finds his guys all like the other leader better? I had to face my fear that the guys might like Brad better and want to follow him rather than follow me. That was irrational since we're all on the same team, but most pastors have seen it happen, if not within their own church, then certainly with the church down the street that has the hip pastor and the cool crowd. We are shepherds; part of what comes with that is to be jealous for our flock. It is easy to take a self-righteous attitude and let insecurity, or envy, ruin it. But in my family, running from a fight was considered an act of cowardice. I couldn't see a way to win without taking the risk.

I set out to get to know Brad and give him an idea of how I did things and how I'd like for us to work together. We were more than a little wary of each other, but we were both committed to God's kingdom and both sure the church is God's vehicle for changing the world.

I can't remember now all the things we did to create a friendship, but I do know we drank a lot of coffee. Brad was a strategy, plan-and-attack kind of man. I am rather a fly-by-the-seat-of-my-pants person. I have always had trouble spelling organized but have come to live by a schedule. So we talked.

Not, mind you, so much about men's ministry, but rather about our views of life, family, church, worship, and discipleship. Brad was very intentional about discipleship—he was in the Navigators after all—an organization that trains people to share their faith with others. I am much more casual in my mentoring style. But I was very appreciative of the intentional, well-planned approach and we started with a good base of mutual understanding.

We started with the obligatory men's breakfast at O-dark-thirty on a Saturday morning. Oops, I said *we*, didn't I? It wasn't we, I wasn't there. I work on weekends and they are way too busy to start in the middle of the night with having pancakes. But I did check to see how it went. There were a few hearty souls—guys who obviously liked eating breakfast hours before dawn.

• •

By this time in my ministry there were many books on the market about Christian manhood. Patrick Morley wrote *The Man in the Mirror* in the early 1990s, speaking to what Christian men ought and ought not to be. About ten years later, John Eldredge wrote *Wild at Heart,* which captured the imagination of men around the country, partly, I'm sure, because of that great title. Eldredge claims that men are bored; they fear risk, and they refuse to pay attention to their deepest desires. He challenges

Christian men to return to what he characterizes as "authentic masculinity" without resorting to a "macho man" mentality.

Suddenly there were many books being published with the same kind of drive pushing men to a new level of authentic manhood. This was a different emphasis than we'd seen in the churchmen of the twentieth century. This new push caught the interest of some of the leaders in men's ministries. Some were in our church.

3

TROUT BUMS: OR HOW I GOT DRAGGED INTO THE OUTDOORS

In the undertow of this current, a couple of our outdoorsy guys started a "weekend in the woods" gathering. It was everything I feared about men's gatherings encapsulated in a cold wet weekend.

Are we having fun yet? Well, how would I know? Remember, I'm the guy whose congregation expects him to be in the pulpit every Sunday, or so I told myself. How could I go and get in touch with the wild man inside of me? I had to preach.

So the men went off to the woods. I want to tell you it was a dismal failure. But it wasn't. It showed us that there were men who would show up and enjoy something outdoors in the Great Northwest, even if it was a church thing.

Are we on to something here? I thought, with a bit of trepidation. *I'd still rather spend my time in a soft leather chair by a fireplace.*

In the summer of 2000, Brad and his right-hand man, Jay Huffington, dreamed up an outing for the opening day of trout season. Because of the weather and the number of potential catches, they decided to have it in eastern Washington, about a three-hour drive from Enumclaw. Like the good elders they were, they asked me, "What do you think?"

"Do they still catch trout in Washington? Does it have to be so early in May when it is still so cold? Do any of our guys actually own rods and reels? Can you get enough guys to fill a whole car?" I said along with other obviously helpful and encouraging remarks.

I was only making conversation because: 1) I had never caught a trout; 2) I didn't expect that more than four or five of our guys even knew how to hold a rod, much less unravel a tangled reel; and 3) thankfully I had to preach that weekend and wouldn't share in the pleasure of sleeping on the cold ground in an equally cold tent with the Trout Bums. Nor would I be sitting on a shore before sunup freezing my sizable behind off drowning worms.

I finished the conversation with a hearty, "But hey, sounds like a great time. Why don't y'all give it a try?"

• •

I'm not sure how it happened or what malevolent forces were at work in my life, but after a couple of years of safety, my two oldest grandsons said, "Papa, we want to go to Trout Bums. Will you take us?" Trout Bums Roundup is the official name of the annual men's outing of The Summit.

My oldest son, Bret, had been wanting to get the boys into outdoor activities. He said, "Come on, Pop, let's take your Suburban and join the guys. I want to teach the boys to fish."

I thought I was safe with Bret. He's a data architect who spends his days trying to straighten out the Department of Health for Washington State. He stares at computer screens in warm dry offices and computer labs. For fun, he plays lead guitar for rock bands. He's more often found in smoky rooms with rock musicians than by a clear mountain stream. I had confidence he'd see the wisdom in staying warm and dry and buying fish at Safeway. But no, he played the grandfather card on me. "Come on Pop, it could be fun."

I want to tell you it was the best week of my year, but it wasn't. Oh, I enjoyed being with the guys and having a cigar around the fire and sharing a bit of our lives together. But it was cold and windy. My boys started out sleeping in tents while

We stayed warm by shivering and chattering our teeth.

I slept in my Suburban. But after the temperature dropped to about 28 degrees and the windows on the inside of my Chevy were iced up, the boys ended up in there with me. Sleep was almost non-existent and we stayed warm by shivering and chattering our teeth.

But we had a very large group of men who didn't seem to mind the cold and had a good time. "Fun, eh pastor?"

"Uh, yeah, sure . . . where else can we be so in touch with nature?" *Yeah, where indeed?* In my reluctance, I was more of an anchor than a sail. That's not a position I wanted to be in.

I realized there had been important connections made with guys in the church, and some who didn't attend our church, that couldn't have been made anywhere else. I could see that this was going to be a yearly pilgrimage that was going to have to be endured.

To give you some idea of the significance, we had more guys there that weekend than normally attended church any given week. We usually had about 125 men in attendance on Sundays. At Trout Bums we had more than 150 guys. I would have never guessed.

I was witnessing a phoenix rise from the campfire ashes. I saw men who were marginally involved with our church take on huge responsibilities in providing and preparing food and organizing games for the younger men. I discovered we had retired special forces guys who spent three days setting up and teaching rappelling, rock climbing, and field navigation. I realized we had resources that would never have been revealed in small group Bible studies or tea and cookies after church. I was blown away with what God was showing me. And all in the context of men being men, doing what they liked to do, and bringing other men into the fun. I witnessed a level of camaraderie I had never before seen in a church—any church—and I'd been in church all my life.

> *I was witnessing a phoenix rise from the campfire ashes.*

Did I go again? Yeah, you betcha. But the next year I took my wife's travel trailer. And the die was cast.

4

ISI, CHUCK STECKER, AND AN OLD BLUE MERCEDES

I have attended a million conferences in my life, give or take six. Some have been great and helpful, some have not even been a good reason to leave town. So when Brad came into my office and said, "There is a perfect conference for our guys called Iron Sharpens Iron (ISI). They're holding it in Lakewood. We need to get all our guys to sign up."

I was underwhelmed. In Lakewood? This city about twenty miles away from Enumclaw was not known for drawing great conferences.

"All day Saturday?" I asked. "Has anybody heard any of these guys speak before? Have they ever spoken anywhere before? If they are so good how come they're speaking there?"

"It's a national group and they have great speakers," Brad said. "You heard one of them in Orlando at the National

41

Coalition of Ministries to Men conference. You remember Chuck Stecker, the retired military guy with the great voice?"

Oh, yes, I did remember Chuck Stecker. Part of our Joshua's Men's leadership team was going to the NCMM conference. They told me, "It would be great to have you with us. We've got extra air miles and we'll room together so it'll be cheap." Secretly, I think they bought one too many nonrefundable tickets and needed someone to fill the seat, but that's not what they said. Not being a big conference fan, and never having heard of the NCMM, I hesitated. But, I wanted to be with the guys so I said I'd go.

I had no idea what to expect but when I got there, I was impressed with the NCMM. It may well have been the best conference I'd been to since the Congress on Biblical Exposition in Houston a decade earlier. These guys had a handle on the issues facing the twenty-first century church.

After looking at the schedule, it was hard to decide which breakout session to attend. I ended up in a classroom that was totally full—I mean guys hanging out the windows and sitting on the floor and all. I almost went to another class and probably would have except I couldn't get out of the room. I was glad I'd limited my coffee intake that morning.

Then Chuck was introduced. He was everything I hated about conference speakers. He was bigger and better looking than I, was a retired Lt. Colonel, had a doctorate or two, was obviously smarter than I, and had the kind of voice every preacher in the country would kill for. But despite his shortcomings, he won me over with his insights into the problems facing men in the church.

Now he was going to be in Lakewood at the Iron Sharpens Iron conference just about an hour's drive from my office. "Okay, I'll go. Sign me up," I told Brad. Ah, but as you might imagine by now, that wasn't the end of it.

Brad said, "Hey, Chuck is available to preach at The Summit the day after ISI. Why don't we invite him to speak?" I wanted to say, "You're kidding, right? You want me to invite a guy I hardly know to speak from my pulpit?" But I didn't.

I very rarely invite guest speakers onto our stage. Very rarely means hardly ever, as in maybe a couple of times in thirty years. I am very jealous for that time and space and protective of the flock God has assigned to me. Yeah, I liked Chuck as a speaker for men, but would his message resonate with the whole church? That's how I was talking to myself. I am afraid I was thinking he was going to force me into areas of ministry I didn't have time for, or more probably, was not competent in. Somehow he brought out all my insecurities and my sense of dysfunction. It wasn't his fault. It was God dealing with me.

As I was wrestling with the idea of it, I drove by the local Starbucks and saw Brad and Jay sitting out front having coffee. I couldn't put this off any longer. I had to decide and this was the perfect time. I pulled in and joined them for coffee. I honestly couldn't think of a good reason not to have Chuck speak. I tried to think of something that wouldn't sound lame. But my thinking was lame so how else would it sound? So I told the guys, "Sure, let's have Chuck come and speak. What harm can it do?"

Jay said, "Great, it'll be fun." Oh, yeah, I've heard that before.

On the weekend of my first Iron Sharpens Iron conference, all the guys from our church who were attending met early Saturday morning. We had an old bus and a van we were taking. Since I had to be back at the church before the conference was over, I was driving my car to the conference. Since Chuck would be preaching at The Summit on Sunday, we got him a hotel room in Enumclaw. So he was there as we were filling the bus. I motioned to him and asked, "Do you want to ride with me?" He did. I had no idea how my life was about to be changed in a thirty-minute ride in an old blue Mercedes sedan.

Conversation flowed as we drove in the pre-dawn darkness. He was easy to like. Our families were about the same age, we liked rock 'n' roll, and we both had a desire to serve the kingdom of God. But he had an enthusiasm for ministries for men that was catching.

That weekend, being with Chuck and other men's leaders and speakers revealed a world of ministry opportunities I had heretofore missed or shied away from.

Watching men of my church come together in a unified effort for the kingdom of God reshaped my future ministry.

I saw for the first time what I would see a dozen more times in the coming years. When a group of men from our church worked together to put on a conference that was not focused on our local ministry, I saw the bond created and a closeness and chemistry that could not be produced any other way. It happened to be at an Iron Sharpens Iron Conference, but it didn't have to be ISI; it just had to be a kingdom thing in which they were more than spectators. Being with Chuck, who was on the inside of the conference leadership, allowed me an inside spot, even if for just a short time.

Catching the vision of men like Brian Doyle, Pat Morley, Robert Lewis, and Chuck Stecker shook my ministry world. Watching men of my church come together in a unified effort for the kingdom of God reshaped my future ministry. I became, and shall evermore be, a supporter of ministries to men. But I didn't yet know my part. There was no need for me to start a men's ministry at our church. Brad and his warriors already had Joshua's Men up and running—pretty much without me, or at least with minimal effort on my part. I was not resistant but passive.

It would take me some time to find what God wanted and what Joshua's Men needed from me.

5

SHOWING UP

What did Joshua's Men need from me?

As the new ministry began, I was happy we had a guy to lead it and a few men to attend. I don't know what I expected from this ministry. I kept tabs with Brad and talked to some of the guys about what was going on. I saw the pictures they took of their outings and I spoke about it with appreciation from the pulpit. It was not a great surprise to me that it was sparsely attended; that's what I expected. I'd never seen a men's ministry that drew too well.

Every now and again, Brad would drop hints to me about attending. "Hey, why don't you join us this Saturday for our breakfast? We'd really like it if you did."

I had good reasons why I couldn't. I was, after all, a very busy guy. At 7:30 Saturday morning? Finally, I ran out of excuses.

Not just to the guys, but to God. You remember Him, he's in the Book.

A strange thing began happening. I kept awaking about 6:30 each morning there was a gathering. *Okay, I'll go once in a while. I can't commit to every time though, that would be too hard on my schedule. You understand, right?*

But He didn't seem to.

All right, I'm going, I'm going. I started attending. It was good, very good. They had challenging speakers and interesting topics. Who knew we had guys in the neighborhood who were so gifted? I even started going on the outings. Not all the overnighters; no need to overdo it, eh?

The few guys who went seemed pleased I was there. I don't know why. I didn't teach. I didn't do much of anything but show up.

Then an amazing thing happened. Oh, you're way ahead of me, but yes, the ministry began to grow. It was exciting to see the growth. They didn't flood in, but each time we met there were a few more guys. I was a bit incredulous. *How is this happening?* The ministry hadn't changed. I watched with great interest. What were they doing that made the difference?

Brad scheduled a team leaders' meeting and asked me if I would attend. "You don't need to speak or jump in on the planning session, but it would be good if you'd be there."

> *"You being there validates the ministry."*

"Sure, I can do that." Sounds like a deep commitment, doesn't it? Yeah right, but I went and we had coffee and some food and we talked about the ministry. They talked, I listened.

Then during a break I asked a simple, innocent question, "Why do you think we're seeing such an increase in the interest of the men?"

"It's you," they said. "It is because you are there."

"Uh, but I'm not doing anything; I'm just there."

"That's the point," Brad said. "You being there validates the ministry. If you attend, it must be important. It must be worthwhile."

• •

In case you haven't picked it up, I'm not what one would call an attractor. If people who know me need an illustration of something average, they could use me. I am average. Average height, average build (well, for a pastor, we often run toward the chunky side), average intelligence, and so on. Average. People don't flock to me.

I had an associate pastor of worship who was an attractor. He could draw a crowd. I remarked once to some people about the difference.

They said, "No, pastor that just isn't true. He is younger and better looking, but we don't think people are more drawn to him."

Church people sometimes go out of their way to be nice; they lie, but they are nice. We had a Christmas party coming up the next week. So I said, "Watch how people react to him."

On the night of the party, I stayed on the opposite side of the room from my associate. My witnesses were shocked. As people came into the room they greeted me and moved over to talk to Roger. He was an attractor. I am not. It's okay, I'm not bitter. I tell this story to show you that the increase in the ministry was not because I was there and everyone wanted to be with me; it was because the senior pastor was there. They didn't come to be with me, they came because if I was there, it must be important.

• •

I told you about Trout Bums and my being dragged into the outdoors. What I didn't say is that when I started going, it took off in numbers. It was surprising to me then. It isn't now as I've learned what the senior pastor participates in has a different value to men. If the pastor doesn't go, why should they? If it isn't important enough for the pastoral staff to attend, it must be optional for them too.

This will not be at all surprising to some. You might be used to having an entourage wherever you go. But this might be new information to others. You are the guy I want to talk to. I am the living example of what Dr. Lewis was talking about at the Reload 2014 Conference. When the ministry to men wasn't important to me, it just meandered along. When I started showing up, most of the men in our church did too.

So how about you? Pastor, are you in the game? If not, you are in the way.

PART II

We Have a Problem

6

· ·

WHAT'S WRONG WITH THE PASTOR?

Here's how I see the problem of what is lacking in pastors.

He is unaware of the great value of one.

I've told you how I got dragged into ministry for men, not exactly kicking and screaming, but kind of. Is my story unique? Not according to what I hear at conferences and seminars. I may be a bit eccentric—okay neurotic—but more pastors are like me than not; ask Robert Lewis.

What is it about us pastors that makes us resistant? If *resistant* is too strong a word, how about hesitant to jump into men's ministries?

He doesn't know what he doesn't know.

It is hard to imagine there is a pastor in this age who doesn't recognize the need for a ministry for men. There has been a concerted effort by many organizations in recent years to educate the church and its leaders to the need. But knowing it is a good idea, and recognizing the need in the local church might be different.

I had read many of the popular books, but having never been a part of such a ministry, I didn't fully comprehend how great the need was. I grew up in a church that was reasonably populated by men and surely had many programs that were men-oriented, but there was not a specific focus on men. At least not one that was obvious.

I was not taught in college or in seminary about the great potential lying dormant in our churches. I was a firsthand witness to the feminization of our congregations. I was steeped in the axiom that if it hadn't been for the women, the American church would have died out a hundred years ago.

I think we just took it for granted that men were not very interested in church and what we had to offer. I'm sure there were those who saw it as a problem; many, like me, just accepted that this was the way things were and always would be.

Even Bill Gothard, in his Institute for Basic Youth Conflicts seminars, said if we had the choice of discipling men or women, we'd be wise to work with women first. His reasoning was that if we discipled the men and their wives disagreed with us, they would undo what we were doing with the men. I guess he deemed the men too apathetic or passive to resist their wives, who were seen as more spiritual.

> *We didn't know what most men wanted, but we thought we did.*

That was the prevailing attitude and one I held. I had pastored a couple of small churches and I had seen firsthand that men were more difficult to attract and disciple than women. Right or wrong, that was the way it was. Like generations of pastors before me, I thought since most of the active members in my church were women, they deserved the most attention. We'd get to the men later, I supposed.

It wasn't as if we didn't have anything for men. Well, now that I think about it, we didn't, but we *thought* we did. We had Bible studies and discipleship groups and some outings from time to time. They weren't well attended. Honestly, we wondered why. We had good "manly" material. We had nice men leading them and we had coffee and cookies. What did these guys want?

That was the missing piece. We didn't know what most men wanted, but we thought we did.

He doesn't know how to begin.

Before I met Brad Stewart and Chuck Stecker, I attended a Promise Keepers rally. PK created an awareness of the potential that a ministry for men offered. Like most pastors, I had read the books. But I was busy with the church so I didn't do anything about it. Ah, now that is a cop out. Sure, I was busy, all pastors are, so are the men in the congregation. It makes a good excuse for why some vital things never get done. The truth is, I didn't know what to do so I put it off for some other time. Lots of important things get put off because of that.

I need to make a confession that is painful. I wasn't a disciple-making pastor. Just as with men's ministry, I read books on discipling and even attended some conferences and seminars on the subject. I knew I should be and I wanted to be. I could talk the fight lingo, but honestly, I was not in the battle. I had some guys whom I was training and guys around me who were growing in their faith; I even participated in some discipleship programs. But they were largely that—programs. I hadn't been discipled myself and I had never been taught how to do it. It is said, experience is the best teacher; when it comes to making disciples, I believe it is true.

How would I start a ministry I wasn't confident I could lead? I could start another program but I knew that wasn't the way. I sure didn't know how to do it successfully. I had never been a part of a ministry for men and I had never seen one that worked.

I'd heard about them and read about them but never had the opportunity to participate in one. Honestly, the idea scared me. Where would I start?

Pastors are supposed to know everything and be the guy who has all the answers. This is a mind-set that easily besets young pastors even though we know it's not true. It takes a certain kind of ego for a person to stand up each Sunday and demand, well ask anyway, for everyone to stop what they're doing, sit down, shut up, and listen to him. We know we don't have all the answers, but we are not at all sure we want our people to know it. Our people want us, maybe even expect us, to be that person. I, for one, wanted to be that person.

> *We know we don't have all the answers, but we are not at all sure if we want our people to know it.*

I was expected to know how to disciple men, individually and in groups. I was a pastor, for goodness sake, and that is what pastors do. But as I just said, I *didn't*. And I was not mature enough or secure enough to admit that and get help. How does one confess that he is the only pastor in the Western world who isn't good at making disciples of men? And even if I were inclined to acknowledge my deficiency, who would be my confessor?

So the cycle continued. I'd buy the latest book on the subject and attend a conference led by a guy who pastored a church of two hundred million, earned his first Ph. D. at eighteen, looked like Robert Redford, had a voice like James Earl Jones, drew applause when he sneezed, and could leap tall buildings with a single bound. I would listen, take copious notes, and realize I wasn't that guy and would never be able to do what he'd done. I'd go home, write my annual resignation letter, and sink into depression. Later, I would tear up the letter and put the whole idea on a shelf with my unwritten novel, half-done dissertation, unfinished series on Revelation, and hopes of being the next Chuck Swindoll. Then I would get on with the busyness of being a small-town pastor. A ministry for men would have to wait.

He is afraid to take the risk.

"Everything you've ever wanted is on the other side of fear," said George Addair, an American businessman from the last century.

Not knowing what is needed is understandable. Not knowing how to begin is excusable. But knowing what needs to be done and being afraid to do it is sinful. Fear is a non-active faith.

I have participated in the planting of two churches in my life. One took, one didn't. In baseball that's batting 500, not too shabby. But in life it's only a 50 percent success rate. After the first failure, I was sure I would never do that again. "If at first you don't succeed, try, try again," was not my motto. "If at first you don't succeed, try something else," is more my speed. Risk is fine for skydivers, rock climbers, and venture capitalists, but for average guys, remember, *average*, it keeps them up at night.

> *Fear of taking a risk is a bigger problem than we'd like to think it is.*

George Addair was right. What we want is always on the other side of fear. I don't know whom to blame for that, probably that rascal Adam, the gardener. Do you know why every time an angel showed up he said, "Fear not!"? Because the person to whom he was speaking was about to die of a massive coronary. I know for a fact if an angel ever shows up to speak to me, he's going to want me to do something I will find scary. I'm not sure that him simply saying, "Fear not," is going to make it all better for me.

Franklin D. Roosevelt said in his first inaugural address, "The only thing we have to fear is fear itself." Yeah, and looking real stupid in front of people who pay us to lead them in all things spiritual. I love to read about Joshua and Caleb. They were *men*. But remember, God had to tell them to be brave and of good courage. For them, the Promised Land was also on the other side of fear. They just didn't let that stop them.

Fear of taking a risk and jumping into a ministry for men is a bigger problem than we'd like to think it is. As pastors, we

> *Your pastor may look like a fearless warrior, but often it's a professional facade.*

can have all sorts of reasons—read excuses—but the fear of failure can stop us in our tracks. Unless we face it.

Men, your pastor may look like a fearless warrior, but often it's a professional façade. It's not a mask he intentionally wears, but a necessary part of his leadership toolbox. I'd be the last one to say he's a phony, he isn't; he is a flesh and blood man who has the same insecurities that most men have buried. But he, being God's anointed, doesn't feel free to express his anxiety for fear of being judged as weak or unspiritual. We'll get to how you can help later. For now, it's enough to know that not feeling free to express his anxiety can be part of his reluctance to get on board a ministry as messy as one for men.

But wait, there's more. The average pastor, and the non-average one for that matter, is used to being in control. I mean, that's part of his job description.

Many years ago, I went to a conference where Bill Hybels was speaking. I hate *that* guy. Not really, but he brings most of my deficiencies to the surface. Did God have to make him so handsome *and* smart? Anyway, he was speaking on leadership. He said many of us, as pastors, shouldn't be the leaders of our churches because we aren't strong enough. He was saying we should find another guy more suitable to take the lead. We should just study and pray and leave the leading to that other guy.

"Oh!" you might say, "that's not what he meant." Maybe not, but then why were there fourteen guys in the men's room looking like they were going to the gallows? Maybe he didn't say exactly that, but that is what many of us heard.

We are called to lead and paid average bucks to do the same. To admit we might not be the strongest leader, phooey, to even *think* we might not be an adequate leader, is a major downer. And then some other guy wants to step in and take control of a major part of our congregation. Is it any wonder that often our first reaction is, "Hell no!" Only we're pastors and seldom use that term if we're not talking about Satan's house.

Are we control freaks? Sometimes, but not always. Most of us are willing to relinquish some of our pastoral responsibilities to another guy. But it can be awfully hard.

I'm going to be talking about what's wrong with men who would be men's ministry leaders in another chapter, but we must address the two-bulls-in-one-corral thing. The standard image of the successful pastor is of a type-A, choleric extrovert with a bass voice, heavy beard, and hairy chest. For those of us who aren't any of those things, we learn to act like that. It isn't that we're faking it; it is that there are expectations of us that we must live with, like it or not.

It is sometimes a blatant fear of losing control.

It is, admittedly, sometimes a blatant fear of losing control. And that is, as you are probably thinking, sin, plain and simple. But there is more. The senior pastor is responsible for his flock. Every pastor I know feels that deeply. The buck stops with him. He knows if he lets go of the reins and all goes badly or people get hurt, he's going to be at the end of the pointed fingers. And most of the fingers pointing towards him are his own. He is going to blame himself for the failure. Is that bad? No, it comes with the job title.

Yes, sometimes we're just jerks and can't let others be in control. Sometimes we are afraid people are going to like the other guy more than they do us. Fine, I said it. And it is true. There are some pastors who are "ball hogs." There are some who honestly feel they have all the answers. If there is to be a successful ministry for men, they will have to lead it. Their ego won't let them play a support role. They aren't right to be like that; it isn't godly. But another man with a superego who mostly feels the same way is not going to find easy sledding on that slope.

Pastors are men with egos, insecurities, control issues, and a strong sense of responsibility, all of which can be perverted and lead to unrighteousness. They are not to be ignored or accepted as normal in their corrupted forms.

Ah, but the man who starts or takes over a ministry for men is subject to the same temptations. While two heads are better than one, two heads are also the basic ingredients for a fight.

He needs help we don't have.

During the time between my first PK rally and when The Summit had its first real ministry for men, I was in a quandary about what to do. I didn't know what all to do, but I did know I would need a faithful and devoted guy to take the lead. At that time, I didn't have that man, and I wasn't confident I could build him.

When God provides the guy, it is intimidating.

When Brad Stewart showed up, he worried me. Why? Well, I didn't know him. But it was more than that. He intimidated me. No, that isn't true, he did nothing to do that. I was intimidated by him. It was on me. He wanted me to do something I knew I should be doing but wasn't. He was pushing me to do what we needed and I don't like to be pushed. That is not a good response from a pastor. I knew that.

It is true that I didn't know Brad very well and that is not a good thing on which to start a ministry. A working partnership must be based on some level of trust that we had not yet developed. We had some work to do.

So why was I intimidated? Can we examine that for a bit? I had worked hard to start this church. I had invested untold amounts of time in developing relationships and programs I believed would strengthen the body. But that isn't all. There was a level of insecurity on my part. Brad was a strong personality and had years of experience as a master chief in the navy. What if he did a better job and the guys liked or respected him more than they did me? He *would* do a better job than I because I hadn't done anything. Anything he did would be better.

Is it completely wrong to be concerned that another man would damage what had been worked on for so long and so diligently? No, but to block a needed ministry because of worry that it would make me look bad is most assuredly wrong. I should have been excited that he wanted to get such a vital ministry started. But I was fearful. If I was just fearful that another man would mess things up, I could possibly justify my fear. But I was afraid of being shown as being incompetent. And that is sinful.

7

WHAT'S WRONG WITH THE MEN'S MINISTRY LEADER?

We've acknowledged that there may be a problem with the senior pastor. But does all the fault lie in his corner? Yeah, maybe. But for the sake of discussion, let's look at some of the issues from his point of view.

The would-be ministry leader is not under authority.

Imagine this scenario with me. There are two guys, Pastor Fred and a man named Mike. Fred pastors a church that Mike attends. Fred has been there a number of years and the church has been moderately successful. That is, the bills are paid and more people join than leave. It is a good church. Nice people go there and Pastor Fred preaches the Word faithfully. People are happy there. There are more women than men, but Fred has hope that more men will join eventually. His strategy is to work harder at what he is doing and pray God will send more men.

Mike has attended Fred's church for a while now. He sees there are more women than men and it bothers him. He thinks it should be otherwise. He thinks Fred should do something about this and right now. Mike thinks, *If Fred isn't going to fix the problem, I should step in.* Mike decides he should start a ministry for men.

Mike goes to see Fred. "Pastor, we need more men in our church. We aren't attracting good men. I read David Murrow's book and I see what we're doing wrong. You just aren't doing the right things to get men in the door. If you'd read the book we could fix this. And I have others you need to read."

Mike has never been in ministry. He has read a few books on leadership and he's been to a couple of rallies for men. Mike is a sales executive for a machinery company and has experience supervising people, mostly men. He has a reputation as a man who gets things done. He does leave bodies in his wake, but hey, "Go big or go home" is his motto. Persistence is a quality Mike possesses and he is proud of it.

What Pastor Fred heard Mike say was, "Fred, you aren't doing much to get men into the church and what you are doing is all wrong." To be fair, that isn't exactly what Mike said, but to be honest, it *is* what he meant.

Mike likes Pastor Fred just fine. He thinks Fred is a good preacher and does religious things with some style, but, Mike is not impressed with Fred's leadership. In Mike's mind, Fred should be more forceful at business meetings and speak out more forcefully on issues Mike thinks are important. He has been heard to say, "Fred would never make it in the business world; not aggressive enough." Oh, and he has also been heard saying, "What can you expect, Fred only works one day a week, har, har."

Fred likes Mike. He recognizes his sales skills and his strength of personality. He knows of Mike's reputation for getting things done at any cost. Fred would like to have someone take responsibility for a ministry to men. Is Mike the one?

So Fred says to Mike, "I agree we need such a ministry. I don't have a lot of experience in this, but I have read some very good books and I have an idea of some strategies that might work with this church in this community. Why don't we meet weekly, study some books together, and come up with a plan to get this thing off the ground?"

"See, that's your problem. Fred. You want to overthink everything and make plans. Let's just do it. How hard can it be? We have some men's breakfasts, plan some fishing trips, and get some football player to give a talk. As a matter of fact, I've taken the liberty to schedule some events for this month. Invitations and notices have already gone out."

"*Trust me, it'll be great. Just leave it to me.*"

"Those are all good things, Mike, but we've not discussed them with the board, and we've not checked the church calendar for available times and places. I don't want to overthink, but you're right, I think a good plan needs to be in place. Some coordination with other ministries in the church is in order. We want to get started right. We need to have a plan. And while it may sound religious, some time invested in praying over it wouldn't hurt either."

"Phooey. I think we should get the ministry started now. We can fix it along the way. You and the board don't have to waste time with plans and strategies, I'll make it happen. Trust me. It will be great. Just leave it to me."

. . . .

This is fictitious, to be sure. But I have heard variations on this theme many times at pastors' conferences. I use this to illustrate some of the problems that pastors face from men who would be leaders in the local body.

Mike represents a serious flaw in men's ministry development. First, he doesn't respect his pastor's position or authority. Mike doesn't dislike Fred, nor does he want Fred's job. Mike thinks Fred does a decent job in the pulpit, and as a smiley face in the church on Sunday, he acknowledges Fred is above average. If he were asked, he'd say, "Yes, I respect Fred and I'm glad he's the senior pastor."

But Mike has an attitude problem.

Mike thinks he could lead the ministry for men better than Fred. That isn't the problem; he probably can. Mike can see the ministry is not what it could be and he has a strong sense he can do it better.

Fred is not leading a ministry focused on men for many or all the reasons we talked about in previous chapters. But Fred is the senior pastor. He has been anointed by God to lead the flock. Mike doesn't respect that reality. Mike doesn't understand that Fred is God's man in that church.

Mike sees Fred as an obstacle to getting the job done. He's ready to work around him, work through him, or go over the top of him to start a needed ministry. God bless him, I appreciate his enthusiasm and passion. What makes matters worse, Mike is partly right. Fred is an obstacle. But Mike is wrong in thinking it is his job to start the ministry anyway, despite Fred.

Mike has concluded that it has become his job to fix the situation. He's run out of patience with Fred and just wants Fred to get out of the way so he, Mike, can get on with God's plan for the men of the church.

If we won't take no for an answer from those over us, we set ourselves up to miss the "no" from God.

Fred is a problem, no way around that. But Mike's "charging bull" approach has removed him from being part of the solution. His unrighteous disrespect for Fred's office has taken him out of the game.

Mike's disregard of Fred's position creates a chain reaction. Now that he believes Fred doesn't know what to do, it must mean that he, Mike, has all the answers. Pride sets in. It's a subtle thing. When we believe we are the man with the plan, we are not only closed to the leading of the people God has put in authority over us, it also closes us to the leading of the Holy Spirit. If we won't take no for an answer from those over us, we set ourselves up to miss the "no" from God.

Mike became an entity unto himself. He doesn't mean to be opposed to God, but that is what pride does to us. When a man is willing or wanting to work around the people God has put into place, he is unwittingly working around God; teachability is destroyed or greatly diminished.

Here's my take: If a man will not accept the authority placed over him, God will not put him in a place of authority over other men. We'll talk more about that later.

In my fictitious scenario, I've made Mike a good-hearted man gone wrong. Mike is not a wicked man who is intentionally circumventing God's program. He truly means well.

> *There are men in our churches who don't want to be leaders, they want to be king.*

But there is another kind of man I've seen who moves in to start or take over a ministry. This is the man who would be king. He is another problem for the making of a ministry for men.

He wants to be king.

Being a leader of men can be a macho thing. Men watch *Braveheart* and want to be William Wallace standing before blue-faced men and calling them into battle. What man hasn't imagined himself in such a place, being such a man. It appeals to the ego, to our pride. There are men in our churches who don't just want to be leaders of the King's men, they want to be the *king*. These are men without the Spirit. And let me tell you, if you don't already know, Spirit-led pastors will have an aversion to this man. The pastor may not even understand why he feels as he does, he just does. And the man who is the would-be leader, and the men he draws around him, will see the pastor as just another obstacle to establishing his own kingdom.

Their goal is not to start a ministry for men; their goal is to form a club that will let them be president.

Pride can be such a hidden master. Unspiritual men don't know they are unspiritual; they don't recognize they are seeking to build their own kingdoms; they just feel the vacuum and are drawn in by the possibility of being somebody.

There are a couple of types that fit this. One is the man who is used to being the boss, the man in charge. He probably has a strong personality and is a natural leader. It feels right to him to draw the men of the church to himself.

The second type is the man who has never been the leader. He isn't a natural leader but the role appeals to him. No one has ever made him the team captain and he longs to be. When he sees the possibility, he jumps in. Neither of these types wants to lead men to Christ; they want to pull men to themselves. Their goal is not to start a ministry for men; their goal is to form a club that will let them be the president. They won't make the church or the men of the church strong but will pull these men out of the body and weaken it. Every pastor is going to resist these men. To some, it may appear as if he is standing against a ministry for men.

The subject of this book is overcoming the obstacles to starting a ministry for men in the local church. Dr. Robert Lewis says the senior pastor is the primary obstacle. I don't disagree. But the guy who would be the leader of such a ministry can also be a major obstacle. The reason for the pastor's reticence may well be his own inner conflicts, but we must not miss the fact that the reason for his reluctance can be what he sees in the man, or men, who want to start this ministry.

But there is a fix. We'll deal with that.

PART III

The Fix

8

. . . .

JEFF AND DALE

I want to tell you another story. My story about Fred and Mike was fictitious; this one is real.

Let me introduce you to Jeff. Jeff is a bull of a man. He has big, big hands, big arms, and a barrel chest. His graying hair and beard and the crevices etched into his face reveal the miles he's traveled. Jeff has worked many jobs and has had a couple of careers. He has always been a hard worker and inevitably floated to the top and became the leader. He's used to it. He likes it. He's good at it.

Jeff looks like a football player—well, one in years now gone. By his own admission, he liked football because it allowed him to hit people. Yeah, that kind of guy. He likes Harleys and a good cigar. He especially enjoys them with his pastor. Yeah, he is *that* kind of guy.

Jeff grew up in the church but like a lot of men, kind of outgrew it as he got older. About twenty years ago, Jeff became part of a local church just down the road from me. After settling in, he joined a men's Bible study. The group was small, just him, his pastor, and another guy. The group had been larger, but after the pastor introduced them to Pat Morley's book, *The Man in the Mirror,* the group diminished. The men in this church were not ready for such deep introspection and left the group—not the church, just the group.

Jeff, his pastor, and this other guy were meeting together weekly and studying Scripture and sharing their lives together. Jeff, trying to keep his expanding girth from expanding too far, walked a trail every day. On the trail one day, as he was walking and chatting with God, he heard God say that the little Bible study needed to expand and draw other men into it. Jeff even heard the new group should be named Men of Faith, as it had been called in its previous incarnation.

Being a man of action, Jeff immediately went to see his pastor and told him of the impression he'd gotten from God while he was walking.

Jeff's pastor's name was Dale. Well, it still is actually, but I digress. Let me tell you about Dale.

Dale is Pentecostal from the word *go*. He was raised in a Pentecostal preacher's home and he's been pastoring Pentecostal churches since he was a kid. Dale is a type-A personality, a combination of choleric and sanguine traits. Whatever he does, he does with gusto. Bold is a word used to describe him by his friends. Brash is sometimes used by his detractors. He has been at his church for more than thirty years so, yes, he has some detractors. He loves Jesus, loves his church, and loves to preach—again, with gusto.

Dale believes men of God ought to be men of integrity. He tells his people they should know their strengths and weaknesses, and own their own stuff, and especially applies this to men. To be truthful, he doesn't always use the word *stuff*.

In hearing the story of their foray into Pat Morley's book, it was obvious that not all the men in his church wanted to be as introspective as Dale thought they should be, hence the downward growth of the past men's group.

"If they don't want to deal with the truth, they can go away. I'll spend my time with people who do," is the way he describes his attitude. Dale is that kind of guy—bold, brash, and passionate about following Jesus.

It sounds like a war in the making or at least a loud battle. Jeff, the guy who liked to hit people on the football field, and Dale, the preacher who believes men ought to be all in or get

Get out the mop and pail, Martha, there's gonna be blood on the floor.

out. Get out the mop and pail, Martha, there's gonna be blood on the floor.

But that isn't what happened.

"Pastor Dale, you might not believe this, but I was just walking and praying. I've heard a word from God. He said that you need to revive the men's ministry, and I'm supposed to help you."

"Great, let's do it," Dale said. "Start getting the guys together. We'll do this as a team."

This sounds more like a made-up story than the one about Fred and Mike, because this isn't the way it usually happens. I want to contrast the two stories, compare the attitudes and actions of all the characters, and see what there is to learn.

9

FIXING THE PASTOR

We have looked at three scenarios. One was my history. One was a composite of men I have seen over the years. And one was about men I know. My story was one of hesitancy and reluctance. The composite pastors were also hesitant to begin a ministry for men, even opposed to it. The third was open to it, willing to jump in. We've discussed the problems with the first group so I will only mention them in passing while attempting to highlight what the correct approach should be.

Be cautious, but listen for God's leading

There are three attitudes behind the senior pastor being an obstacle to starting a ministry for men. The first is fear, which I'll detail, the second is concern for the integrity of the ministry, and the third is his desire to see the right man in the leadership role.

Fear. I hate to use that word. I'd rather use caution, concern, worry, or something less severe. You can if you like, but for me fear is the appropriate word. Caution is a good thing. We all should use caution in our ministries. Concern is also a good thing, though probably less so than caution, but both words lead to acting a certain way without necessarily stopping us from acting altogether. Worry is somewhere between caution and fear, but since we're told not to worry by Scripture, it is not a good thing. Fear, my choice of words, leads us to inaction; it keeps us from doing much of anything. And that is the problem we're most directly addressing.

As pastors, we hold two things very dear, our reputations and our jobs. There are obviously many other things we cherish, but in vocational ministry these two stand out. Having someone point out a deficiency in our work threatens both of them. And this is usually our reaction to someone wanting to do something we aren't doing, as in the case of a man wanting to start a ministry for men. If we were doing it, he wouldn't be there pointing out our fault.

So when we feel like our reputations or jobs are threatened, how are we supposed to react? If we are truly men after God's heart, what would we do? What should I have done when Brad approached me; what should Fred have done when approached by Mike?

Don't see the other man as a rival.

To start, Fred and I should not have become defensive. In my case, there had never been a better time to start the ministry than when Brad showed up. I might have missed some opportunities in the past, but that is the glory of following Jesus—I can repent and move on. That is what I eventually did, but my first response should have been to grab the opportunity God was presenting. I should have been cautious and careful, to be sure, but not resentful about someone wanting to do what I was not doing.

God was offering our church a chance to do something significant. Why did I need to get the praise? Was my reputation so important that I couldn't let someone else get the pats on the back? I guess it was but it shouldn't have been. My job? The folks in the church didn't care if I was the lead on this or served as support staff. Truth be told, the men thought more highly of me because of it. Stupid, I was just being stupid.

Grab the opportunity with both hands.

Because of my stupid reaction, I missed recognizing at first that God was doing something He wanted to do. If He had walked in and said, "Ross, I want to begin a work under your ministry and I want Brad to lead it," what would I have said?

"Yes, Sir! You got it. Whatever You want. I serve at Your pleasure."

If you remember my story of Jeff and Dale, that is what Dale did. He was not fearful of what others might think of him—he jumped in.

Turn the men loose; they aren't yours.

But, but, these are my men. I worked hard to get them to this church. What if they like him better than they like me?

There is my insecurity showing and a whole lot of my pastoral brethren. It doesn't diminish my weakness to recognize it is a problem for a lot of us. It can be considered an occupational hazard because pastoring is such a part of our lives and hearts.

Let's see, are they *my* men? I may have worked hard to get them, but do they belong to *me*? You know the answer. So if they are not my men but God's, why am I being possessive? If this other leader is being sent by God, can I trust them to Him?

Relinquish control, accept leadership.

What if this other guy won't follow me? What if I can't control him?

To start, if he won't follow, then he shouldn't be in leadership. That's where the caution comes in. But controlling him is another issue. Letting him take the lead will diminish your control absolutely, but who said *you* were

Control is God's; leadership is our gig.

supposed to control? Leading and controlling are not the same. Demanding to be in control is not the attribute of a shepherd—it is the cowboy syndrome. Control is God's; leadership is our gig. I know, some pastors feel the need to micromanage everything in their churches, but very few have the bandwidth to pull it off. If the pastor must control his disciples, are they learners or servants?

Some, like my friends Jeff and Dale, become co-leaders. Jeff was given the title of men's ministry director with a great deal of latitude. Dale was right there with his sleeves rolled up, willing to do what needed to be done.

You might ask, "Isn't it possible this guy could run the ministry into the ground? Couldn't he damage the church?"

Good questions. Yes, he could, if you aren't involved in the program.

Show up; be involved.

If the pastor chooses to be a spectator and not be involved, then yes, it can go south before he knows it. That's why the pastor *has* to be involved. When I began attending all the gatherings in my church, not only did it increase participation by the men, it gave me firsthand exposure to what the leadership team was doing.

I was going to title this book, *Just Show Up*, based on a Chuck Stecker sermon. Of all the things a senior pastor needs to do to ensure the success of the ministry, this is the most important. One cannot lead what he isn't a part of. Pastor Dale agrees with me completely. Whenever his guys gather, if possible, he is there with them, not to control but to participate. As a participant, he has firsthand knowledge of what's going on and can immediately jump in and be a part of whatever corrective action might be needed.

While the primary focus of this book is getting a ministry for men started, a good foundation will go a long way towards the maintenance of it. The integrity of the ministry and of the lead man is vital. The senior pastor must watch both. It is his responsibility.

Stay in constant communication.

Just showing up is important, but the importance of staying in close communication with the lead man or the leadership team cannot be overstated.

We had a situation arise in our ministry. Brad, whom I've told you a lot about, was working as a trainer for IBM. His job required him to travel every week to some far-off place. And as you might imagine, when he was home on weekends I was not the person he most wanted to spend his valuable time with. Odd, huh? Well, anyway, our communication dwindled down to almost nothing. We did e-mail back and forth and that was helpful, but times over a cup of coffee or a cold beer stopped.

I didn't think too much about it. But then I noticed there were plans made and acted on that I knew nothing about. They weren't bad things, and I trusted Brad, but it became a bit embarrassing when people asked me questions about things of which I was totally unaware. Before IBM, Brad was at every elders' meeting and everything was openly discussed. Brad is an idea guy and always had several ideas that he and I would discuss and that were presented to the rest of the men on the board. That became impossible with him being away so much.

It wasn't too long until Joshua's Men, our ministry for men, began to feel like a para-church ministry. It didn't feel connected to the church body. And it wasn't. I still participated, but I no longer knew everything Brad was thinking or planning. A major point of contact had been lost. Both he and I felt the disconnect. It was going to damage the ministry.

> *It is imperative that the senior pastor and the lead man for the ministry for men be always connected.*

We finally decided that his second in command, Jay Huffington, would take the first chair and Brad would step back.

It is imperative that the senior pastor and the lead man for the ministry for men be in constant communication, always connected. The senior pastor needs to know what the ministry leader is thinking and the man leading the ministry for men needs to know the thoughts of the senior pastor.

Being in close communication has an added benefit. People have issues in their lives. Some of those issues can lead a guy into places he shouldn't be and things he shouldn't do. Being in close personal communication elevates the possibility for accountability. When we spend time on a regular basis, any changes the other guy might be experiencing will more likely be detected. I'm sure you've noticed how body language, facial expressions, and verbal tones are very revealing of what a person is feeling or thinking. As helpful as electronic communication or social media might be, those revealing characteristics are missing. Hints that something may be wrong are impossible to detect in an e-mail or even a phone call. Nothing replaces face-to-face interaction.

As a recap, here's my take on fixing the pastor.

1. Be cautious, but listen for God's leading.

2. Don't see the other man as a rival or a competitor.

3. Grab the opportunity with both hands.

4. Turn loose of the men; they aren't yours.

5. Relinquish control, accept leadership.

6. Show up, be involved.

7. Stay in constant communication.

10

FIXING THE MEN'S MINISTRY LEADER

Are you the guy who wants to present his desire to start a men's ministry to the senior pastor of your church? If so, I want to teach you some things about how to approach him successfully.

So far, all the fixing has been done to the senior pastor, and I agree that is where the fix must start. He is the head servant in the church and bears the ultimate responsibility for what happens in the church. But as the adage goes, "It takes two to tango."

I grew up Baptist and we didn't know what a tango was. We didn't dance. We were told not to have sex standing up for fear it would lead to dancing! We changed the saying to, "It takes two to fight," because we *were* allowed to do that. We turned that into a fine art.

Join with him before you ask him to join with you.

And that is what happens too many times when a man first approaches his pastor about starting a ministry for men in their church.

If we're going to ask the pastor to change, it seems only fair to ask the guy who wants to start a ministry to change also. Not only is it fair, it must happen. If you have any hope of actually starting such a ministry, there is going to have to be growth on both sides, or at least a valiant effort to grow. Your goal must be to start a ministry, not to have an excuse for why you were unable to do so.

I have discussed this topic with many pastors, some with men's ministries up and running, some who don't have one yet. These four directives came out of hours of discussions and too many libations to count. But hey, who's keeping track?

To all who would start a ministry for men in your church and are planning on approaching your senior pastor, here are some tips to give you a chance of success.

Consider his position.

Join with *him* before you ask him to join with *you*. In evangelical Christianity, we don't consider every word spoken by the pastor to be *ex cathedra*, that is, we don't believe his words are infallible and absolute truth. We know it isn't good when the pastor makes all the decisions and leads all the ministries. We do believe, however, that he is the one whom God has put in place to be the head servant to His flock. Your pastor has responsibilities to his congregation, and to God, to lead these people. He

Be a part of his ministry before you ask him to be a part of yours.

is accountable to the people and to his denominational leaders, and of course, to God. Please, never forget that while he may be able to speak to God on a first name basis, he is still a man, a flawed man, and you just might be walking into his deepest insecurities and fears.

Like most pastors, he has given flesh and blood for this church and has more than a vested interest in it—it is his life. If you are going to start a ministry within his area of responsibility, you must realize the tension this is going to cause.

These are *his* people. Actually, they are God's, but He has put this man in an anointed position to oversee them. Ultimately, these men will come under your authority also, but that doesn't take them out of his flock. Don't steal these sheep! Don't try to take them out of the flock. You must consider that he, being human and therefore sinful, may well feel as if that is exactly what you are doing. This is the tension you are going to be working under. Your pastor needs to feel as if you are a part of his ministry before you ask him to be a part of yours. Join his support team, or council of leaders, and get comfortable working within his sphere. Participate in the leadership of the church before you branch out into a new area.

Remember, your pastor is going to have to give an account for what takes place in the church, and that includes responsibility for you. I want to say this in the strongest possible terms: If you don't recognize you are a man under authority, or if you can't lead under that authority, then you are not the man to be leading a ministry.

Include him in your planning.

In our case, Brad turned out to be much better at planning than I. His training and experience made him a natural at building the foundation and strategizing the development of this ministry. But you can bet I wanted to see his plans and strategies before he began implementing them. In my experience, most pastors don't want to micromanage, but we don't want to have to dig ourselves out of a hole that someone else has dug for us.

It is harder to correct a ministry gone awry than to build it on a solid foundation.

Anyone who has been in the pastorate more than a few minutes knows it is harder to correct a ministry gone awry than to build it on a solid foundation to begin with. So draw up your goals and make your plans, but include your pastor in the foundation building. You may have great goals and a brilliant plan, but if he doesn't feel he has free input into them, you are going to have a tough time making them work.

Stay in constant communication with him.

A ministry to men in the local church must not be, or even *feel* like, a para-church organization. Let's face the facts. If you are a guy who feels called to start a ministry to men, you undoubtedly have a strong personality to go with that. So does your pastor. That is going to create tension. And it should. Have you heard the adage, "If two men agree completely on everything, one of them is unnecessary"?

If God puts it in your heart to start such a ministry, He has given you ideas and goals that are necessarily somewhat different from what your pastor has in his mind. In this case, two heads are better than one. But this is not the situation where the left hand shouldn't know what the right hand is doing. Ah, communication. It seems so elementary, but it often isn't. It takes time and effort to keep others informed about what you feel God wants you to do.

It is not sufficient for you to file your business plan and then copy your pastor on what you are doing. He needs to know constantly and consistently not only what you are doing, but also what you are thinking. Time consuming, to be sure, frustrating, without a doubt, and bothersome at times, but absolutely necessary. You *do* need him to be your advocate. You need him to support what you are trying to accomplish.

I know of nothing that will foul a ministry faster than the ministry leader and the senior pastor not being on the same page. And nothing will protect that from happening more profoundly than being in constant communication.

Listen to him.

Yes, I know, your pastor is not Pope Fred, or whatever. But he probably has been around the block a few times and has learned some things along the way. He certainly does not have all the answers, but hey, that's why he has you, hmmm? And unfortunately for him and you, you don't have all the answers either, or you'd be the pope. Am I right?

The Bible teaches there is wisdom in the counsel of faithful men. Your pastor is familiar with the dynamics surrounding your church. He has knowledge of things that, I can assure you, you don't. He is an asset to your ministry. Use him. Tell him what God is telling you, then listen to what God is saying through him to you. I don't mean just *hear* what he is saying, I mean listen,

listen to his words and to his heart. Maybe he isn't Solomon, but now and again there will be real wisdom in his thoughts and ideas. Pay attention.

> *Your pastor has knowledge of things you don't. Listen to his words and to his heart.*

I wish I could say that doing these four things: considering his position, including him in your planning, staying in constant communication with him, and listening to him, will guarantee your ministry success. Alas, it will not. But it will help you overcome what is said to be your major obstacle in getting it started.

I was such an obstacle. These things worked to win me over. Joshua's Men became a thriving ministry at The Summit in Enumclaw, Washington. Of course, many other things were needed to make this ministry a success. But for that to happen, it had to overcome me—you remember—the obstacle.

11

. . . .

YOKED TOGETHER

Teamwork requires certain things from each part of the team. To be successful, each player must excel at his position. That's basic. The primary leadership team in any ministry to men is the senior pastor and the men's ministry leader. There will be others on the team as it develops, but these two are the start. I want to explore what it takes from each man to make the team great. One man cannot make the team. If we are going to create and maintain a ministry to men that will be significant and world changing, the leaders of the group must rise above the average of what we see in modern masculinity. The "just-good-enough" approach will not cut it. If we accept mediocrity from

If we accept mediocrity from the leaders, the ministry has little chance to be the power for change that God desires.

the leaders, the ministry has little chance for the impact it could have, indeed the power for change that God desires.

Paul's instructions to Timothy are surely words that must be applied to any candidate for such a leadership position. But there is a bit more I'd like to address, not because of my wisdom, but because I heard an expert on leadership speak these thoughts and I would like to add them.

Leading men is not easy. There are some who have done extraordinarily well. There are some who have led men into impossible situations and have prevailed. I think most often about military leaders.

On Veteran's Day, everywhere I look I see the faces of men and women in uniform valiantly serving this country. Especially profound are the faces of old men who served in wartime. They look so old and frail but I know they were once the roughest, toughest fighting force the world has ever known. The names George Patton, Doulas MacArthur, Dwight Eisenhower, and others come to mind. War demands great leaders of men. Men follow strong leaders.

There are other names like Hitler, Mussolini, and Stalin that also come to mind from that period. Evil men could get other men to follow them. Some followed because they had a gun to their heads but others followed willingly and gladly, even into doing atrocious acts.

• •

Maybe men aren't so hard to lead, if one has the right stuff. I am a fan of the Global Leadership Conferences that Bill Hybels hosts each year over satellite connections. One year I heard him say there are three attributes he seeks when bringing in new leaders, three things he looks for his leaders to possess. They are: character, competence, and chemistry. These are the attributes the pastor and the men's ministry leader need to possess in ever increasing measures.

Character

Character is defined as the aggregate of features and traits that form the individual nature of a person; it is his moral or ethical quality; it is an account of the qualities or peculiarities of the person.

It doesn't always seem that political or national leaders must have any good character traits to lead men in the world at large. Men will follow a "strong man" if he can convince them he has a place to take them. He can be a man totally devoid of any moral character. Indeed, he can be a madman. I offer some of the men mentioned above as exhibit A. Hitler moved a whole nation toward his own goals and changed the face of Europe and millions of lives forever. He was the personification of evil. But men followed him, even to death, willingly and enthusiastically.

A man with only the appearance of godly character might be followed.

It could be this way in the church. A man with only the appearance of godly character, but with enough enthusiasm or charisma to enable him to take charge, might be followed. I am sure we've all met the person who could pull this off. That is surely one of the fears that can keep a pastor so cautious as to be inert. It would be easy to say, "The men in our church would never follow a man without good character." But haven't we all seen leaders in the church, even pastors, who are more concerned for their kingdom than for God's? And we've seen good-hearted and well-intentioned people support such a leader completely. How can that be?

We can all be deceived.

There are too many godly character traits listed in Scripture to be listed here. For our discussion, however, there need be only nine. They are found in Galatians chapter five. They are listed as the fruit of the Spirit. It seems almost silly to say, but I must. Anyone in leadership, especially of men, must be Spirit-filled.

Anyone in leadership must be Spirit-filled.

I don't want to get caught up in the baptism of the Spirit argument, I just want to say, that anyone, anyone in leadership, must display the fruit of God's Spirit at some level.

You might say, "I know that, nothing new here!" The voice of reason would say, "Then why are there so many jerks in church leadership?" And you know there are. How did they get there? Somebody wasn't paying close enough attention, that's how. Somebody missed something in the process. There is no other explanation.

Oh, wait, there is another explanation. Maybe this person started his own ministry and was not under the authority of a godly pastor or other godly men.

I know, I know, nobody consistently displays the fullness of the fruit of the Spirit all the time. But Jesus said you can recognize a tree by its fruit (Matt. 12:33) and "This is to my Father's glory, that you bear much fruit, showing yourselves to be my disciples" (John 15:8).

Is there spiritual fruit, or isn't there?

What are we looking for? What is godly character?

Love

I said this before, but here it is again: A man who would lead men must love the guys. Simple, but not so easy always to do. Some guys are just not easy to love. Some are downright hard to even like. You know I'm right. A man who would lead men must enjoy hanging with the gang. It needs to be more than a time to endure, or a platform for his self-elevation. The man God wants to lead will be like Jesus in that he will choose to be with his guys every chance he gets. Just watch the dynamics of a gathering. It doesn't take Sherlock Holmes to figure it out. According to Jesus, people will know this person is a disciple of His by this trait, by his love for the men under his care.

Joy

The leader we want for the ministry is going to enjoy doing it. It is going to give him pleasure; he's going to be energized by it. Yes, it can be exhausting, but Jesus experienced that too. It's the overall picture we're interested in. Is this guy having a good time serving God in this way? I think it is possible to fake loving the group for a short time, but it's hard to look like you're having fun when you consider the whole thing to be a drag.

Peace

To me, peace is more what he brings to the table than what he feels in his life. Does this man cause dissention or disunity? Do you see him in tension with other guys all the time? Is he a peacemaker among the brethren? Is this guy constantly in conflict with somebody? This is a sure sign he is building his own kingdom. If it doesn't go his way, he's unhappy. A bad choice.

Patience

Yes, we're getting personal now. Most men, especially men who get things done, are not known for their patience. There are times when what appears to be patience is just passivity. Is the difference knowable? I think so. The man who is frustrated with something not getting done, but is by character a patient man, will be moved to action. Not to do it himself, but to help the person responsible get it done. He may show his frustration but will be quick to take responsibility and repent. The man who is frustrated, even angry, but is passive, will just stew about the failure to comply and get bitchy. He will become resentful and blame everyone else for their failure.

What of the man who lacks patience? He will show himself quickly. He'll always be angry because he will always be frustrated, and he will show both in time. Hard to miss chronic impatience in a leader.

Kindness

To my mind, this is a composite trait. The man who is loving, joyful, peaceful, and patient will be a kind man. He will treat the men under his leadership well. He will not be easily angered or inappropriately frustrated. He will be understanding of others' flaws, and he will treat them as he wants them to treat him. We've heard that one before, eh?

But we must not see kindness as an excuse not to confront sin and hold men accountable for their actions or lack thereof. The man we want in leadership will be kind and gentle in rebuke. Look for this trait, as it requires strength to confront gently.

Goodness

Does the man wanting the position, or whom you want for it, display integrity, honesty, and compassion? If so, he's a good man. This too is a composite of what comes before in Paul's list of spiritual fruit. Can one truly be good without the other examples of spiritual fruit? Can he be good and not loving, or good and not a peacemaker, or good and not kind? These are self-answering questions.

Jesus said there is none good but God, and that is difficult to argue with. But it makes our point. Without the Spirit of God, there will not be the kind of goodness we're seeking. Yeah, it's true, we've all met nice guys who were not followers of Jesus, men who did not possess the Holy Spirit. But we're looking for godly goodness, not just a nice guy with a pleasing personality. It's hard to tell the difference I know. That is why we need godly discernment to know by which spirit the man is motivated.

Faithfulness

Faith in God is, of course, necessary. Being faithful to follow Jesus is mandatory. But there is more. Isn't there always? We need to see a faithfulness to the ministry and to the guys the leader shepherds. Is he faithful to get the job done? Is he faithful to do what he says he will? Is he faithful to consider the needs of the other men before his own?

This is where the tire meets the track. A man can be the nicest, most loving, peaceful, and all the rest, but if he isn't faithful, he's the wrong guy for this job. I'm not sure where I'd put him in service, but surely not into this demanding position. The men's ministry leader must be a guy known for his follow-through. All the time, every time? Of course not; no one is *that* faithful. But what's his reputation? Is he known as a man who gets things done? Do people know he is a man who keeps his word? What about his relationship with his family? Is he faithful? Don't let a man who doesn't show a Spirit-given faithfulness anywhere near leadership of men. He can't be trusted.

Gentleness

This is basically kindness. But Paul listed it separately, so there must be a difference. What do you think? Some have defined gentleness as: the character that will show calmness, personal care, and tenderness.

Let's look to Scripture for some clarification. Paul writes in 2 Timothy 2:24–25: "And the Lord's servant must not be quarrelsome but must be kind to everyone, able to teach, not resentful. Opponents must be gently instructed, in the hope that God will grant them repentance leading them to a knowledge of the truth."

Paul puts gentleness in apposition to quarreling, which will not bring people to the truth. Paul is concerned that disciples be able to bring people to the truth. Not by arguing, but by gently persuading, gently changing another's heart. That is definitely what we want as a leader of men, one who is gently persuasive and able to change people's hearts. I like that. I think I'll leave this in.

In 1 Thessalonians 2:7, Paul says, "But we were gentle among you, like a mother caring for her little children." Many of us came to Christ at the knee of our mother. She didn't use power or strong words, did she? Not mine. She gently told me the truth, and because of her gentleness, I was drawn to believe her. That is a good example of the kind of guy best suited to lead our men to following Christ.

Self-control

The Spirit leads us to control ourselves. We all know working with people, especially men, can make us crazy. Well, can't it? People are the most confusing and frustrating things on earth—well, next to old Chevys and computers. We can replace those things, but people are our purpose. We can't replace them. We have to work with them and be of service to them, even when they are problems.

The man to lead our ministry is necessarily a man under control. He will have the attributes the Spirit gives or he'll be harmful to the group, especially if he is unable to control his temper, his anger, and his actions.

Let me finish this section by saying we are all a work in progress. But we need to have progressed a bit before we take on shepherding others and taking responsibility for them. Paul warns about putting a novice into a position like this. Makes perfect sense.

COMPETENCE

Competence is defined as the ability of an individual to do a job properly. Competency is a set of defined behaviors that provide a structured guide enabling the identification, evaluation, and development of the behaviors in individual employees.

Ability to do a job properly. Competent to lead. To be able to convince men to do or go where one wants them to go. Manipulation and leadership often look similar. The big difference is whether the place being led to is a good place for

> *The man may be as spiritual as an apostle, but can he lead men?*

the follower to go and whether it is good for him to be there.

There is also the issue of what the person being led understands about the journey. Is he going there willingly and knowingly or is he being intentionally deceived about the destination and the journey?

Competence, then, may be the talent or skill needed by a man to persuade men to accompany him on a journey to somewhere. A man may be as spiritual as an apostle, may have enough gifts to last him several lifetimes, but can he lead men? Maybe he has memorized the New Testament, maybe he can recite the Apostle's Creed in Latin, maybe he has led dozens of people to Jesus, but can he lead men? Being a scholar, a soul-winner, even a great teacher, doesn't mean he is the man to create, lead, or maintain a ministry to men. They are good and great abilities or gifts, but they do not make a man competent to lead men. They just don't.

Having read every John MacArthur book printed would surely be a good thing, but does the potential leader have any experience? Does he have a track record of being a leader? We might have a man who has proven himself in other areas that we believe gives him potential. I get that. I think that is good. But then, who is going to walk along beside him to be his mentor while he is learning this ministry? There will need to be someone watching the development of competency.

Unlike character, competence can be taught and learned.

Unlike character, competence can be taught and learned. Then we are going to have to know this man's teachability. Is he willing to say, "I don't know," or ask for help? We are all required by God to be growing in our competence as we serve. None of us is as good as we can be. There will always be things we don't know. That's a given, isn't it?

Even a guy just starting to lead must have some level of competence. Do you know what that is? Do you have requirements for the man, expectations of his abilities? Can you articulate them? Are they published? Does he know what you want or what you require? Being able to do the job well is the goal. Is there a plan in place to help a man get there?

CHEMISTRY

I have worked in multiple staff churches for most of my ministry life. I have worked with all kinds of people in all kinds of ministries and situations. To have a successful team there must, must be chemistry. I heard Dr. Hybels say we can compromise a bit on competence, if necessary, but not on chemistry. I don't think Hybels cares if I agree with him, but I do, absolutely.

Without chemistry we don't have a team, we just have a group of people trying to do the same thing. It is subjective, I know. It may be hard to define, but oh my, you know when it is there, and you feel it when it isn't. Before I talk about getting the person that "fits" with the team, allow me to discuss chemistry.

How do we know when we have chemistry? We know we have it when we have:

- A oneness of goal and purpose.

- An appreciation of the giftedness of the team members.

- A knowledge that together the team is greater than the sum of its parts.

Oneness of goal and purpose

I am convinced that in order to establish whether there is chemistry, you must have defined and articulated goals and know your purpose.

Can I get personal for a minute? Can you articulate the goals you have for your pastoral team? I know there have been long periods of time when I could not. If you can't, it's going to be very difficult to know how the men's ministry guy is going to fit in. If you are in the process of starting this ministry, or you have a guy bugging you about it, this is for you.

When we started our men's ministry, I didn't have a clue what to write as a purpose for a ministry to men. I knew we wanted to win men to Jesus and disciple them, whatever that meant. I knew generically what church ministries were about. In our case, I was blessed to have a guy who was further along in that than I. He had the goals. Not the ideal, but it is workable if there is room for discussion and compromise when negotiating the goals. We were so blessed. I listened to his goals and purpose and found there was little to disagree with. We passed the first chemistry test.

Appreciation of the team's giftedness

I am grateful I was taught the team leadership concept early in my ministry. It was partly because I knew the area in which I was not gifted and would need help. It did take some bumps to figure them out; maybe I'm still learning. But I knew I couldn't effectively do all the things people expected a senior pastor to do. So I got help. I was blessed with great team members, some who worked with me for twenty-five years, almost unheard of in ministry circles.

I also learned about spiritual gifting early. I was taught how the gifts basically worked, how to help others determine their gifts, and how to fit them together in ministry, both vocational and volunteer.

I knew I needed help, and that together we were stronger, smarter, and had a greater opportunity to develop the ministry.

When Brad came to start a ministry to men, I knew what to look for in a leader of men, well, at least academically. I had a lot to learn about Brad's gifts and he mine. We came to appreciate each other's giftings. It wasn't hard work, but it took some in-depth conversations. We came to know what to expect and how to approach problems.

We found we had many likes and dislikes that were the same and had some pastimes we could enjoy together. We took full advantage of those pastimes and our friendship and brotherhood increased.

Knowledge that together the team is greater than the sum of its parts

For me, understanding this was the easy part. I was coming to see and know what I hadn't known before. I knew I couldn't start, or manage, a good ministry for men. I was only adequate and that is the anathema of great.

I learned that from Jim Collins. To get this job done we were going to have to get the right guy in the right seat, as Collins would say. I knew, instinctively or prophetically, that I needed help and together we were stronger, smarter, and had a greater opportunity to develop the ministry.

With Brad, or Jay, the two ministry-to-men directors I've had, I didn't have to compromise anything. They were men of character, competent men, and we had and still have chemistry. Once I got into the game, even though I was out in left field, God built an incredible ministry through the guys He sent to participate.

12

· ·

ARE YOU THE GUY?

So you have a burning in your soul—or a strong desire—to start a ministry for men at your church? There are some things to think about. Is there a need for one? Are you sure you are the one to do this? You may be one of those guys we discussed after listening to Dr. Robert Lewis at Reload 2014 who want to start a ministry for men but your pastor isn't on board. Maybe you have been praying and waiting for a good time to approach him and lead him into righteousness, well, at least convince him to let you start the ministry. Before you go into his office and become his worst nightmare, let me ask you two primary questions with some minor ones thrown in.

Are you convinced there is a need?

Why do you want to start a ministry for men? Can you articulate it in 100 words or less? There are dozens of very good books about the necessity of a men's ministry. Have you read any of them? Do any of them translate into your neighborhood?

What I want to know is, why do *you* think there is a need in your church? What have *you* seen or heard that convinces *you* that this must be done? Has God given *you* a vision for this, or does it just seem like a good idea?

What do you hope this ministry will accomplish? Do you have plans and goals? Can you recite them at will? Do you think about them often? I strongly suggest you have your plans and goals written down before your pastor asks you about them. Does anyone else see the need? Are there others who feel the same way?

Are you confident in your call?

Why do you think so? I have always applauded an entrepreneurial spirit and a holy ambition, but it takes more than ambition to lead the King's men. I'm not sure one has to have a supernatural call from heaven to lead a men's ministry, but a guy has to have some kind of idea that this is what God wants him to do. My friend Jeff, whom I wrote about earlier, felt a supernatural call. Not everyone does. But I'm convinced it must be more than a passing thought after an anchovy pizza and a couple of beers.

Are you a good follower? Do you have the time to invest? How is your spiritual life?

Do you have the ability or necessary skills to take the lead on this? I'm not too sure I could pinpoint exactly what ability or skills are necessary, but for sure you need to feel you have the stuff if you are going to attempt it. Are you a good follower? Alexander the Great wouldn't have a man take a lead position in his army until he'd proven himself to be a good follower. It's not Scripture, it's true, but it sure seems like good advice to me.

Are you sure you have the time to invest? Are you willing to do so? How does your family feel about it? Is your wife okay with you being so involved? How do you feel about working hard and not seeing immediate results? Are you easily discouraged? How is your spiritual life? We'll talk more about this, but can you say it's good now? Improving?

If you see the need but don't feel you are the man to take the lead, then pray, pray, pray that God will raise up that guy and stand back. Don't be the guy who wants to start a ministry but isn't willing to get his hands dirty. Don't go to your pastor and tell him he should start a men's ministry. I believe if God has put it in *your* heart that *your* church needs this ministry, then likely *you* are the guy to take the lead. Are you in or in the way?

Okay I'm in, now what?

The most effective men's ministry leaders I've ever seen were not vocational pastors. It doesn't take a theological degree to start and lead this kind of ministry. It certainly wouldn't hurt, but it is not necessary. I know there isn't just one kind of ideal personality or character profile for every church. I've seen all kinds of men with a wide variety of skills and talents and a variety of personalities lead successful ministries. But there are some attributes necessary to have in some portion.

You must love God and enjoy being with other men.

Do you love God? Let me just say, if your primary reason for wanting to lead a men's ministry isn't to serve and please God, then you are wasting everyone's time. It isn't that you have to be a spiritual giant, but you do have to be following the Spirit to have any hope of leading men toward a serious walk with Him. How is your prayer life? When you attempt to lead men, you're going to need it. Do you tithe? Jesus said where a man's treasures are there you will find his heart. To lead a ministry for men a guy must put his heart into it. Where you put your treasure is where we'll find your heart.

A ministry for men must be about shepherding men into a greater walk with God. If you want to lead men toward walking with God, you are going to have to be living that life yourself. You needn't be the apostle Paul, but having some success in your own spiritual life is a must. I've known guys who were only a little bit ahead of the group, but ahead

> *The call is to be someone who leads, not herds from behind.*

for sure. Leading must be done from the front. The call is to be a shepherd, someone who leads, not herds from behind like a cowboy. If you just want to gather a group to be pals with, then join a gym.

Do you identify with the guys you want to lead?

The man who would lead a particular group of men has to be somewhat like them. I once pastored a church that was filled with hunters and fishermen. I mentioned before, I come from San Francisco. I didn't, and still don't know much about hunting and fishing. I am not opposed to such sports but I was never taught how to do it. These guys lived and breathed the out-of-doors. I knew which end of a gun to point but I had no proficiency in using one. For me to put on camo and attempt to participate in the hunt as anything but a learner would have been absurd. I certainly wouldn't have been able to be an equal in their avocation, nor could I take a leadership position in their favored activity. I could lead the church but I needed other guys to head

You must be able to talk their talk. You gotta fit in.

up the men's ministry. I wasn't one of them in that regard. They didn't want to discuss books and I couldn't seriously enter a conversation about what caliber was necessary or how many grains of powder to load a bullet with.

If you are going to lead men, you must be able to talk their talk. You gotta fit in. You need to be, to some extent, "one of the boys." In the church I now pastor, we have a group of Harley riders. I like bikes and have spent some time on them, but I don't own a Harley. I do have an elder and a son who are members of the Black Sheep Motorcycle Ministry. I let them carry the water with these guys. I hang out with them, but most of the serious mentoring is done by others.

My friend Chuck Stecker speaks at our church nearly every year. Chuck was a career military guy. He draws crowds and everyone loves to hear him speak. But he has a special ability to talk to the veterans in the crowd. When he speaks at one of our men's meetings, every vet in the church makes sure to attend. He resonates with them. They understand him. He knows their language and has lived some of their experiences. He can share "war" stories with them.

The director of ministries for men doesn't have to be a veteran to minister to vets, and he doesn't have to be an avid hunter to minister to gun nuts, but there must be a level of identification, a certain kinship, to get deep into their lives. And it has to be more than superficial if there is to be the kind of bonding we're seeking.

> *There must be a level of identification, a kinship, to get deep into their lives.*

Yes, there can be a special bond based solely on our relationship with Jesus. But be forewarned, that it is the hard way around. The reason is many of the men you are going to want to lead into that deeper relationship are novices in all things spiritual. They are not going to understand much of that language. They are not going to relate to your passion for Christ and be inclined toward the leading of the Holy Spirit in the same way you are. That kind of relationship seems better in a one-on-one setting than a group.

All things are possible with God. I'm always looking for the most effective and efficient way to lead men.

Are you *all* in?

Working in men's ministries is hard. When done right, it is going to be messy. A superficial approach will only work for a while and it won't accomplish what it needs to. To work with men and lead them into this deeper relationship with Jesus, one must

Being unwilling to be honest about our own struggles keeps the discussion on the surface.

be transparent in his own life and have earned the right to speak into theirs. To speak to a man who is addicted to porn, one doesn't have to be a porn addict but must be honest about the temptations he endures. Being unwilling to be honest about our own struggles keeps the discussion on the surface.

Do you have a redemption story? Are you willing to confess your struggles and able to articulate how God is helping you? Spurgeon used to say you don't have to be a drunk to help a drunkard out of the gutter. But you do have to reach into that gutter to pull another man out. If a man is unwilling to get down into the messiness of another man's life, he is likely to be of little help.

13

MALE SPIRITUALITY

When we talk about a men's ministry, what are we trying to help men become? What kind of men are we working with? What should the twenty-first century Christian man be like? I am smart enough to know we're not trying to make a one-size-fits-all kind of guy, but there needs to be some idea about what a follower of Jesus should look like, don't you think?

In recent years, books describing the American male and why he dislikes, or hates, going to church, or even being a part of church, have proliferated. I think they've done a great job and hesitate to jump in and try to add anything to their work. But, some time ago, I ran into an article that pre-dates all these works. Written by Keith Drury, it was an excerpt from his 1992 book titled, *Money, Sex, and*

> *What should the twenty-first century Christian man be like?*

Spiritual Power. He was deeply concerned about the feminized church. While I see an intentional movement away from this, thanks to Dave Murrow, John Eldredge, and others, most of us are still dealing with remnants of it. I want to use some of his main points to look at what we're working with and what we want the end "product" to be.

I don't know if men have changed that much since 1992, but I'd like to offer my take on what he says from a 2017 vantage point. Dr. Drury makes pointed statements about male spirituality and men in general. He says male spirituality is more aggressive and is visual-spatial and men in general:

- Are less relational

- Are often more informal

- Are warriors

- Carry deep grief

- Are earthy

- Are risk takers and reckless

- Are wild

If he is right, and most of us think he is, then these are the characteristics of the raw material we are working with. When I started in ministry, oh so long ago, I didn't see anyone looking at men in this way. The ministries we had just viewed people as people. There was not, in my humble opinion, much difference between our approach toward men and our approach toward women. I'm sure there were some insightful souls who did approach men differently, but I didn't see it, and I don't remember a single class in college or seminary that spoke to the differences.

I'd like to think every pastor has read the books that have been written in the last decade and have taken this to heart. But I have no assurance this is so, especially if Dr. Lewis is right that senior pastors are still an obstacle to men's ministries. I still see many, many churches with a generic approach to ministry. Maybe I'm wrong; I hope so, but I'd like to add my voice to those crying out to recognize the necessity to do ministry differently when it comes to men.

So if you are one of the "enlightened," rather than take the following to heart, a hearty *amen* will suffice.

Aggressive spirituality

Dr. Drury says male spirituality is more aggressive and spatial. His book says "Words are less important to men than seeing." Some years ago, I saw the line written, "Men don't read." It made me laugh because I was reading it and I'm a man. So it is a generality to be sure. I hope someone is reading this and that he is male. But in general, it is true. Women seem to be drawn to the written word more than men are. I see that in the responses to sermons. Again, I'm talking generalities. But during the sermons in which I use lots of Scriptural references and passages from commentaries or history books, I notice a large percentage of the men kind of float away mentally, while many of the women are busy taking notes. Ah, but when I tell stories, especially about battles or conflicts from the Old Testament (you know there is a lot of gore in the Book), I can usually keep the men's attention. And if I jump around and act them out, I can often get the guys to lean in to hear and see.

In his *Men's Fraternity* series, Dr. Robert Lewis says real men avoid passivity. I guess he means it is a natural thing for men to slide back into passivity in their lives. But I know for certain that men are drawn to people and ideas that are aggressive. So while we as men may struggle with being passive, we are not drawn to a passive Christianity, one that doesn't call us into action, one that is more informative than action-packed.

Remember my story about Jeff and Dale? You'll recall that while the group was just doing Bible study, it remained very small. But when they started calling men into some kind of action, be it outings and events or making real changes in their lives, the group expanded rather rapidly. It isn't that men don't want to know the Bible, it's that it has to be taught in application rather than just the imparting of facts and abstract ideas. Men are drawn to flesh and blood, here and now, let's do something happenings.

> *Men are drawn to flesh and blood, here and now, let's do something happenings.*

Dr. Drury said, "A story or drama communicates better with men than a ten-point 'How to' message." It follows that a ministry to men that is all about *how to do* something, rather than about actually *doing* something, will not attract the men.

Are men *really* less relational than women?

Reportedly, men talk less than women. Many reports say that men talk 40 percent less than women. Is that true in your experience? It is in mine. I'll say it again: Most men would rather *do* something than talk about doing it. This is my complaint about too many discipleship programs—they spend all their time talking about discipling and not doing it. Most pastors and men's leaders know the truth that doing something is men's dominant form of spiritual expression, not religious talking and listening. We've all seen that men's lives change more on a five-day missions work team than during a hundred Sunday services.

Informality and men

A church service that is less formal is going to appeal to more men.

Informality has become a way of life in most evangelical churches. All you need do is watch some of the younger mega-church pastors on television. These super-cool guys have made the standard to be work shirts, skinny jeans with manufactured holes, and a casual setting. A church service that is less formal is going to appeal to more men. Not all, but many. I have friends who have recently begun attending a "high church." The liturgy and formality appeal to them. They like dressing up to go to church. The guys that attend my church are not like that. The men in my world prefer jeans and a sweatshirt with a Seahawks logo over a coat and tie. But it can't just be the appearances. It *has* to be in the feel.

Growing up, my family wore suits to church, even the boys. My father used the line, "If you were going to see the president you'd wear your best clothes." Maybe you've heard this. His idea was that we were going to the house of God and should dress accordingly. When as a teenager I started wearing white Levi's, Pendleton shirts, and sandals to church—yeah, California in the sixties—he considered me very disrespectful, not only to the pastor, but to God Himself. I wondered at times about the passage that says, "Man looks at the outward appearance, but the Lord looks at the heart" (1 Sam. 16:7). Jesus taught on mountain slopes and at the beach. Do you think people dressed up to hear Him speak? Do you think He cared?

A quick story. It was a hot summer Sunday night in Los Gatos, California, when I was maybe sixteen. In our church at that time, the youth of the church made up the choir and we all sat facing the congregation. On this night, we all watched a girl from our high school walk into the foyer. She was wearing shorts, tennis shoes, and a lightweight top. We watched a deacon approach her and have a short discussion with her. She shrugged and reluctantly turned and walked out of the church. We knew what had happened, we didn't have to hear the words. She was not dressed appropriately to attend the service.

I knew her. She didn't know the rules. She was not a church girl. She needed to be in church, she needed to hear a gospel message, but she was turned away because of wearing shorts to church. I don't know if she ever tried church again, but she never came back to our church. That was fifty years ago, and I still remember. Maybe she does too. We were told to win the world for Jesus, but the modeling was, don't bring them to church until they are dressed appropriately. Is that still the message in your church?

I can guarantee you men have attended your church—probably at the insistence of their wives—and never came back because they didn't feel welcome. Maybe there wasn't a deacon

We must do more than accommodate men, we must make them feel welcome.

in the lobby checking out their attire, but did the service say, "Come as you are" or did it say, "Get your life in order, clean up your act and your language, and then come and we'll be glad to have you"? We must do more than accommodate men; we must make them feel welcome.

Men are warriors.

I talked earlier about all men wanting to see themselves as William Wallace. Why? Because men have always been warriors. No, not all men, I know, there have always been the scholars, but even they probably felt that way down inside there was a fighter wanting to get out. It's in our DNA. Get a group of guys together with a cold beer and they want to talk about football or hear the war stories from our vets. At our fishing events, all the teenage guys want to sit at the feet of the pastor and talk

Down inside there's a fighter wanting to get out. It's in our DNA.

about *superlapsarianism.* Yeah, right, in my dreams. They all hang out with our special forces guys or the marines in our group. They do not want to learn Bible stories, they want to hear about surviving Iraq or Afghanistan. They want to learn survival skills or land navigation techniques. Oh, and they want to learn how to rappel off cliffs face first so they can protect themselves from enemy fire.

> *Men around us are carrying deep wounds and experiencing grief.*

At your next men's gathering ask if they'd rather watch *You've Got Mail* or *Braveheart.* Even in San Francisco or Seattle, I'd bet on the result. After WW II, we used to sing "Onward Christian Soldiers." We stopped sometime in the eighties—definitely too masculine. We are in a spiritual battle right now. Are we calling men into battle as warriors?

Men are emotional.

We are told that the American male is not emotional. We all know what to call that. Ha, I wish you knew how much restraint I have been using for the sake of editors. You say, "We don't use that barnyard term around our church." Are you sure you are in the loop? Ah, just saying.

Anyway, it isn't true about men not being emotional. The men around us are carrying deep wounds and experiencing deep grief. Are we expecting them, indeed telling them, to suck it up? I don't know about you, but I'm tired of the cheery feel-good experience that much of the Christian world is selling.

Again, in *Money, Sex, and Spiritual Power,* Dr. Drury said, "We figure that's how we're supposed to run church: 'Aren't you glad to be here on this beautiful day? Turn and shake someone's hand and tell them that you love them,' says the Reverend Mr. Cheerleader. We men dutifully turn, shake, and smile. But we sometimes feel like hypocrites. Some days we aren't cheerful."

In our church, we have law enforcement officers and war veterans who are plagued with post-traumatic stress. They are in your church too. Is there anything in our churches to help them? Do we preach that all that will go away when a man comes to Jesus? Is our ministry for men equipped to help them process? If not, why not?

We have the story of the cross. We follow the Man of Sorrows. We have the Psalms of David in which he laments his life and situation. We have the book of Lamentations in our Bible. Are we drawing wounded men into our fellowship and offering care and understanding? Jesus wept. Are we able to weep with scarred and wounded men? Is there a place for them in our men's ministry? Are we in the game?

Men are earthy.

Did the apostles ever break wind? Oh, come on. Does any man in your church talk like that? Men are earthy, there is no doubt about it. Do we need to always sanitize life? Verily, verily,

I say unto thee, the men you are called to reach use other words. Can you live with that? The men in your town like to sit around a campfire, tell stories, have a beer, and smoke cigars. Ha, you have men in your church who do the same things. Do you ever join them? Would Jesus? You know the answer.

Men are risk takers.

Men do stupid things—or at least what most folks would think was stupid. I have a cousin who used to ride motorcycles on a flat track. His idea of fun was seeing how fast he could go into a turn with the bike sideways and his knee dragging in the dirt. Risk to him was putting everything on the line to beat the other guys doing the same thing. I knew a guy a few years ago who had an idea for an Internet company. He sold everything that wasn't built in, mortgaged everything that was, and put it all on the line to make his company go. Risk to him was doing something better and smarter than anyone else.

Abram packed up everything he had and set out for a place he'd never been. Moses appeared before the most powerful man in the world at that time and told him to turn a couple of millions of his slaves loose. Joshua led an army over the Jordan River and took over a country filled with giants. Peter left his business, changed his life, and eventually stood on the temple steps and accused the men of Israel, and the Roman army, of

> *Are we calling men to take risks for the kingdom of God?*

crucifying the Messiah. Risk takers each and every one. To the world, they were foolish risks.

Again I will ask you, are we calling men to take risks for the kingdom of God or for His church in their locale? Or are we training them to be good little men and behave themselves? I am afraid many of us are missing the mark by playing it too safe and we wonder why the risk-taking men of our world are not attracted to our ministry.

Men are wild.

Keith Drury wrote, "Every man has a wild man inside him." A couple of years ago there was movie called *Wild Hogs*. Maybe you saw it. I've got those guys in my church and in my circle of friends. They are salesmen, programmers, contractors, even preachers by day. Then they put on their cuts (the vest bikers wear with all the patches and letters on them) and they become the Black Sheep Motorcycle Ministry.

About five years ago, before I'd ever heard of the Black Sheep, we held a car show at our church. We put out the invitation to all the local car clubs and motorcycle groups. That beautiful Sunday morning at about 8:00 all these shiny, chrome-covered cars began showing up in our parking lot. Being a car guy, I was

---

out there with our men's ministry guys helping them get parked and set up.

> These guys were outrageous. They were wild. But they were for Jesus.

All was going well when we heard the roar and growl of a group of Harley Davidsons coming into town. There is something about the sound of a Harley. Anyway, the sound grew louder as the group turned into our church. They were a motley group—black leather jackets and chaps, cuts filled with emblems and colors—on very large, very loud Harleys. Long hair, gloves with the fingers cut off, beards, and few missing teeth, in they came. I laughed out loud. What was God up to? It was only as one turned to park his bike I saw written across the back of his cut, "Jesus Is Lord." These guys were outrageous. They were wild. But they were for Jesus.

A bit later they came as a group into our church service. Do I have to tell you the reaction? Silence. But I pastor one of the great churches. Our men's group was walking right behind them talking, laughing, and telling motorcycle stories. The regulars began to walk over and welcome them to our service. Only then did the people see the declaration written across their shoulders. Our folks were incredulous. These guys didn't look like Christians, well not in the traditional sense. But man, could they sing worship songs. It still gives me goosebumps.

Jesus was a wild man, a troublemaker, an interrupter.

Can I tell you something? Almost every man in the church that morning was thinking about buying a Harley. There is something inside of men that wants out, wants to wear leather and roar down the highway. Not you? Seriously? You ever been on a Harley?

Jesus was a wild man. He was a troublemaker, an interrupter. He didn't keep the Pharisees' rules about the Sabbath. In a society that considered women chattel, He treated them as equals. He told the rulers and elites they would be last in the kingdom and preached against the religious bureaucracy.

This wild man went one-on-one with Satan and beat him. Enough with the mild-mannered man with the soft blue eyes and blond flowing hair. I grew up with the Sunday school Jesus who was gentle and always kind and considerate. I like what Drury said, "We met a Jesus who was a nice boy . . . gentle, meek, mild, quiet, vanilla. He was polite, kind, closed the doors after himself, obeyed his mom, always took a bath. He turned the other cheek, smiled sweetly, shared his crayons, talked softly but never carried a big stick. This cozy Jesus never caught a butterfly—he just watched them. He helped his mother, cleaned up his room, never wiggled in church, said nice things to people. . . ."

We were taught that gentle, kind Jesus. Yeah, right, tell that to the money changers in the temple, or the Pharisees whom

He called "sons of hell" and a "brood of vipers." He cast out demons, slept through storms at sea, and wandered around the wilderness with a ragtag group of other guys. Oh, and He withered a fig tree because it made Him angry.

> *Where would Jesus go? Where would He be welcome?*

Thirty-five years ago, I pastored a small church in the small town of Carbonado, Washington. It was a *very* small town. There was a post office, a church, and a tavern. It seemed everyone in town wanted one of them to go away, they just couldn't come to a consensus about which one. One hot Sunday night we had all the windows open. As I spoke, we could all hear the music from the jukebox in the tavern. It wasn't obnoxious, but obvious. I don't recall what I was speaking on, but the thought came to me, so I asked my question out loud.

"If Jesus walked into town tonight, where do you think He would go?" There was a group chuckle and lots of knowing nods. I stood there without speaking for a moment or two as the realization settled in of where the Gospels said Jesus was normally found. He was most often portrayed as spending His evenings drinking wine and having a meal with the sinners and scoundrels of the town. Women of ill repute and tax collectors were comfortable with this wild man. The religious leaders were not because He was just that, a wild man.

A favorite song writer of mine, John Stewart[3] talked about Jesus running with the "hard line gang," and knowing the songs they sang. I wonder if the "hard line" gang in our communities would find a welcome in our men's groups?

Sometimes I wonder if Jesus would.

---

[3] John Stewart, "Friend of Jesus," (Willard: Capitol, 1970).

14

THE RIGHT MAN IN THE RIGHT PLACE

Let's talk about getting the right man in the right place in men's ministry. It is surely an ingredient in the mix of getting a ministry for men started. A fear that the wrong man will be leading it can keep the pastor from supporting a ministry of this nature. If a pastor is confident that the man asking to be allowed to start this ministry is solid biblically, his fear has got to be greatly diminished.

For a pastor, caution and prudence is always appropriate. It is our responsibility to protect the flock. It's our job to get the right person into the right place of leadership or ministry. We cannot simply abdicate our responsibility to accommodate everyone who wants a spot. And most of us have seen that happen. There are some people who want to make a spot for themselves that affords them a place of distinction. Their primary need is not

The best leaders are men who know how to follow.

to see God's church blessed but to feel important or respected. Pastor, you need to guard against that.

There are men who want to lead but are not teachable. We have all known men who had all the answers. They knew how this thing needed to be done and they knew God's mind more than the pastor did. This kind of person is not wanting to work as a team member or even willing to do so. He might even truly know more than the pastor about an aspect of a ministry. But we come back to the necessity of working under authority. The best leaders are men who know how to follow, men who will respect the chain of command and actively work within that command structure. This man also needs to respect the dynamics of his church.

Then there is the guy who says he is willing to work within the command structure but can never take "no" for an answer. Often this kind of guy learned it is easier to seek forgiveness than ask for permission. He is apt to cut corners when it comes to including the pastor or the board. After all, he knows best.

It sometimes is the case that the pastor can be overbearing. There are times when we procrastinate on making important decisions. Or we feel a need to exercise our personality in the guise of being a strong leader. Yeah, we know that can happen and most of us have yielded to that temptation.

The clash of personalities is one of Satan's best tools for negating work in the church. Good men's ministry leaders and good pastors will always be men of purpose. Most always it manifests itself in strong opinions and some arrogance.

> *Arrogance is another of Satan's great disrupters.*

Arrogance is another of Satan's great disrupters. It sometimes looks like two bull elk bouncing off each other in a display of dominance. When I was growing up, we learned on the playground that we couldn't show weakness. Bullies gained their ego satisfaction at the expense of less dominant kids. The church is not exempt from such tactics. Oh, maybe it's not so blatant, but it's there just the same. It can happen under the best of situations with the best of men and intentions. Because of the strong purposes, perhaps it is inevitable at times. But the tension can be exhausting.

Tension that develops between two good men is not all bad. According to Solomon, two heads are better than one. Not exactly his words but the same meaning. With multiple opinions or points of view, wisdom can be formed. But it would be foolish to put a man in a leadership role knowing every decision is going to require a fight.

I'm talking about why the senior pastor is the major obstacle to starting a ministry for men. I am attempting to analyze why that is true. I've been talking about the weaknesses and sin nature of pastors. But there are reasons we have become gun shy. When it comes to men's ministry leadership, I have seen some other things that raise red flags and make us fearful. One is having someone wanting to start the ministry who doesn't have a good plan to do it. Another is having a man who wants to take the lead of men who doesn't appear to have a solid walk with Jesus.

Not yet having a strong plan for the ministry is not problem for the man who is willing to learn and willing to develop that plan with a team. But there are times when a man has a strong desire, righteous or not, to create the ministry but thinks he can develop the plan on the fly. This man may come to the pastor seeking to start a ministry, but he doesn't have a plan for what he wants to accomplish.

I've seen groups form but it was never clear exactly what they were attempting to do. The group would meet and maybe talk about Scripture and have a good time talking about things, but there was little to take away at the end of the time. A group like this seldom maintains life. Before the first gathering of men, someone must have a plan as to what the purpose is and how it can be attained. It's okay if it is untried. It is even okay if it doesn't work. But to start without knowing why is shooting blind and expecting to hit something good.

Another reason for reticence is when the man who would be the leader isn't a spiritual man.

How much spirituality does it take to be a men's ministry leader and how do we test for it? That is probably a whole book in itself, but let's run through some basics.

> *The leader of men's ministries needs to have a deeper relationship with Jesus.*

First, how can a blind man lead other blind men? If leading men to a deeper relationship with Jesus is any part of our goal, then that is where we must start. The leader of men's ministries needs to have a deeper relationship with Jesus. Since this man is going to be a servant of the church, a deacon if you will, it would be wise to see what Scripture says on the subject.

To start, let's look at 1 Timothy 3:8, which says, "Deacons, likewise, are to be men worthy of respect." People must think highly of the leader. That seems elementary. Part of the reason we would pick a guy is that he can draw other men and establish a good relationship with them. What good would it do for a church to have a man leading a ministry whom nobody liked or who couldn't get along with people? Reminds me of the only positive remarks ever made on one of my report cards. They used to say, "Ross plays well with others." In that leadership position, the leader needs to be able to play well with others.

The passage continues by saying he must be "sincere." That is an interesting word. In Latin, the word means "without cracks" or authentic, transparent. He will be flawed for sure; we all are. But does he acknowledge his flaws and seek to remedy them? Has he taken them to Jesus and been forgiven? Does he openly speak of his redemption?

Then Paul said this man is one who is "not indulging in much wine." That seems plain enough. He needs to be a man with his appetites under control. Lots of applications here.

Then he says that this man should be not "pursuing dishonest gain." Again, simple enough, not a thief or a cheat. He must be a man of integrity in every area of his life, especially in his business dealings. That is part of having a reputation other men will respect.

Verse nine adds, "They must keep hold of the deep truths of the faith with a clear conscience." This is not a job for a novice or man with unrepented sin in his life. Taking a place of leadership puts a man in the spiritual war zone. Putting a novice in that spot can set him up for spiritual warfare that he is not yet equipped to handle. Sin in a man's life that he has not repented of opens him up to giving Satan a foothold that can bring trouble into this ministry.

Verse ten tells us men "must first be tested; and then if there is nothing against them, let them serve." I'm likely beginning to sound like a broken record, but it goes without saying that the senior pastor must know this man well. He must not be new to the church or unknown to the leadership. It is best if this guy has served in some other capacities of less weight. If he has served in other positions and done well, then he will very likely serve well here. Makes sense, doesn't it?

> *The character of a man's wife has much to do with his ability to lead.*

In verse eleven, Paul brings the man's wife, if he has one, into the mix. Paul says, "Their wives are to be women worthy of respect, not malicious talkers but temperate and trustworthy in everything." The character of a man's wife has much to do with his ability to lead. If this man hasn't shepherded his wife well, what chance does he have with a group of men? There is a practical side to this. A men's ministry leader is going to know many things that are not common knowledge. In most cases, he will at times discuss these things with his closest confidant, his wife. If she can't keep a confidence, she can severely compromise him and his ministry. He must be able to trust her.

Finally, in verse twelve, Paul says this man "must be the husband of but one wife and must manage his children and his household well." I'll leave the "one wife" thing to each church to interpret, but managing his children and household well is a no-brainer. If the guy chosen to lead this ministry is not a good enough shepherd to manage his household, it would be futile to expect him to shepherd men he may hardly know.

EPILOGUE

So this old cowpoke rides into town after a long trail drive. As you might expect, he stops first at the saloon to wash the dust out of his throat. While standing at the bar drinking his sarsaparilla with his foot on the brass rail—he's a Baptist cowboy—he asks the barkeep, "Where can I get a bath? I need to get the stink of cows off me."

A man cannot be around cows all day and not smell like them.

Same goes for a shepherd. If he is tending his flock, binding their wounds, and walking with them down the paths, he's going to smell like them.

I have a young friend named Marcus. As well as pastoring a small church, he is the police chaplain in our town. In that role, he wears a uniform and a badge. When he's on a ride-along or a chaplain call, he looks just like a cop. The officers know he's one of them. He looks like them, he acts like them, yeah, he "smells" like them. His job is not to preach to them, except when he does one of their weddings, but to be with them as they serve and protect the community. When they are in need, his job is just to show up.

As leaders of men, pastors, and men's ministry guys, we need to be like Marcus. The guys must know we're one of them. They need to know that no matter what happens in their lives, good or bad, they can call on us and we'll be there. Indeed, we have a standard to uphold, but the standard is Jesus, not our self-righteousness.

It's one thing to lead a guy to water, it's another to condemn him for being thirsty. If we hold ourselves apart, we are in no position to help a brother out of a pit or guide him to safety. If we aren't close enough to "smell" like him, we're not close enough to be of much good.

Some of Jesus' friends were fishermen. After a day of fishing, you know they smelled like fish. Jesus wasn't a fisherman. But do you think when Jesus was with them He didn't smell like a fisherman? People knew when He'd been with these guys. He wasn't afraid to smell like them, to be identified as one of them, to eat, drink, laugh, sing, and cry with them. Then He led them to be giants of the faith and they changed the world.

We want to be like Jesus!

ORDER INFORMATION

To order additional copies of this book, please visit
www.redemption-press.com.
Also available on Amazon.com and BarnesandNoble.com
Or by calling toll free 1-844-2REDEEM.